New Directions for Adult and Continuing Education

Susan Imel
Jovita M. Ross-Gordon
COEDITORS-IN-CHIEF

Adult Education and Learning in a Precarious Age: The *Hamburg Declaration* Revisited

Tom Nesbit
Michael Welton
EDITORS

Number 138 • Summer 2013
Jossey-Bass
San Francisco

ADULT EDUCATION AND LEARNING IN A PRECARIOUS AGE: THE *HAMBURG DECLARATION* REVISITED
Tom Nesbit, Michael Welton (eds.)
New Directions for Adult and Continuing Education, no. 138
Susan Imel, Jovita M. Ross-Gordon, Coeditors-in-Chief

Microfilm copies of issues and articles are available in 16mm and 35mm, as well as microfiche in 105mm, through University Microfilms Inc., 300 North Zeeb Road, Ann Arbor, Michigan 48106-1346.

NEW DIRECTIONS FOR ADULT AND CONTINUING EDUCATION (ISSN 1052-2891, electronic ISSN 1536-0717) is part of The Jossey-Bass Higher and Adult Edu-cation Series and is published quarterly by Wiley Subscription Services, Inc., A Wiley Company, at Jossey-Bass, One Montgomery Street, Suite 1200, San Francisco, CA 94104-4594. Periodicals Postage Paid at San Francisco, Califor-nia, and at additional mailing offices. POSTMASTER: Send address changes to New Directions for Adult and Continuing Education, Jossey-Bass, One Mont-gomery Street, Suite 1200, San Francisco, CA 94104-4594.

New Directions for Adult and Continuing Education is indexed in CIJE: Cur-rent Index to Journals in Education (ERIC); Contents Pages in Education (T&F); ERIC Database (Education Resources Information Center); Higher Education Abstracts (Claremont Graduate University); and Sociological Abstracts (CSA/CIG).

INDIVIDUAL SUBSCRIPTION RATE (in USD): $89 per year US/Can/Mex, $113 rest of world; institutional subscription rate: $292 US, $332 Can/Mex, $366 rest of world. Single copy rate: $29. Electronic only–all regions: $89 individual, $292 institutional; Print & Electronic–US: $98 individual, $335 institutional; Print & Electronic–Canada/Mexico: $98 individual, $375 institutional; Print & Elec-tronic–Rest of World: $122 individual, $409 institutional.

EDITORIAL CORRESPONDENCE should be sent to the Coeditors-in-Chief, Susan Imel, ERIC/ACVE, 1900 Kenny Road, Columbus, Ohio 43210-1090, e-mail: imel.l@osu.edu; or Jovita M. Ross-Gordon, Southwest Texas State Uni-versity, EAPS Dept., 601 University Drive, San Marcos, TX 78666.

Cover photograph by Jack Hollingsworth@Photodisc

www.josseybass.com

CONTENTS

EDITORS' NOTES

Since its creation in 1945, the United Nations Educational, Scientific and Cultural Organization (UNESCO) has had a remarkable impact on the world's stage. It was founded "to contribute to peace and security by promoting collaboration among nations . . . to further universal respect for justice, the rule of law and for human rights and fundamental freedoms . . . for the peoples of the world without distinction of race, sex, language or religion" (UNESCO, 1945, p. 3). Promoting these goals through cultural, educational and other means, UNESCO has organized world assemblies and conventions, adopted several international treaties, and developed universal declarations on a wide variety of issues. Perhaps the best known of these is the Universal Declaration of Human Rights—the first global statement about the inherent dignity and equality of human beings—that is now a foundation for a growing number of national and international laws and treaties protecting and promoting human rights.

Adult education has been one of UNESCO's key concerns throughout. With reports like *Learning to Be* (Faure, 1972) and *Learning: The Treasure Within* (Delors, 1996), UNESCO has popularized and promoted concepts of adult education and lifelong learning that are now recognized and accepted internationally. Indeed, in his recent overview of the field, Rubenson (2011) claims that UNESCO's statement of adult education is the most commonly used definition:

> The term "adult education" denotes the entire body of organised educational processes, whatever the content, level and method, whether formal or otherwise, whether they prolong or replace initial education in schools, colleges and universities as well as in apprenticeship, whereby persons recognised as adult by the society to which they belong develop their abilities, enrich their knowledge, improve their technical or vocational qualifications or turn them in a new direction and bring about changes in their attitudes or behaviour in the twofold perspective of full personal development and participation in balanced and independent social, economic and cultural development. (UNESCO, 1976, p. 2)

However, UNESCO has never regarded or advocated adult education as a separate entity in itself but rather as an integral part of a global system of lifelong learning. Indeed, it has probably done more than any other international body to popularize the concept. For UNESCO, lifelong learning should be associated with all dimensions of life, should be possible at all times and all levels and by all means, whether formal, informal, or nonformal (Duke & Hinzen, 2011). This approach to lifelong learning is based on three fundamental attributes: it is lifelong (occurring at every age from cradle to grave), life-wide (recognizing that learning occurs in many different settings), and

NEW DIRECTIONS FOR ADULT AND CONTINUING EDUCATION, no. 138, Summer 2013 © 2013 Wiley Periodicals, Inc.
Published online in Wiley Online Library (wileyonlinelibrary.com) • DOI: 10.1002/ace.20048

focused on learning (rather than limiting itself to education). The success of this approach can be seen in many countries where lifelong learning and adult education are now commonly regarded as synonymous.

Of course, such a perspective is not universally accepted by adult educators: lifelong learning is not just limited to adults; the UNESCO approach significantly ignores any mention of social justice; and it tends to focus on the individual. Some have warned that substituting learning for education can serve to de-politicize the field and shift its focus away from such broader issues as equity, the role of the state, policy, and resources when addressing issues of democracy and equality (Duke, 1994). Most recently, perhaps in recognition that one way to address a proliferation of diffuse, overlapping, and disputed terms is to create yet one more, the recent CONFINTEA VI conference adopted the label *adult learning and education* (ALE; see www.unesco.org/en /confinteavi).

To a large extent, UNESCO's educational work has been channeled and coordinated through its Institute of Education (recently renamed the Institute for Lifelong Learning) based in Hamburg. The Institute regularly conducts studies and produces a wealth of material on many aspects of adult education (see http://uil.unesco.org), including the highly-regarded journal *International Review of Education*. Since 1949 it has organized every 12 years the International Conference on Adult Education (CONFINTEA). Held in Elsinore (1949), Montreal (1960), Tokyo (1972), Paris (1985), Hamburg (1997), and Belém (2009), these conferences have brought together several thousand adult educators and government officials from UNESCO's member countries to review recent developments, debate issues of mutual concern, and recommend policy areas for future adult education research and practice.

The 1997 conference held in Hamburg (CONFINTEA V) was especially significant. For the first time, in recognition that so much nonformal and popular adult education was provided by NGOs (nongovernmental organizations) and professional and community groups, their representatives were formally invited to participate. In addition, CONFINTEA V also "marked a turning point in the global recognition of, and commitment to, adult learning and non-formal education . . . and used adult education as the platform with which to plan for human development within a global context" (Alfred & Nafukho, 2010, p. 95). In particular, CONFINTEA V sought to focus adult educators' attention on addressing the challenges of democracy, peace and human rights, respect for diversity, economic and environmental sustainability, and work force development.

A significant and remarkably utopian document emerged from this conference: the *Hamburg Declaration on Adult Learning and Agenda for the Future* (UNESCO, 1997). Crystallizing the efforts of numerous adult education scholars, international conferences, and civil society organizations through the 1990s, it declared adult education as key to the twenty-first century and asserted the desire to build "a world in which violent conflict is replaced by dialogue and a culture of peace based on justice" (p. 1). Active citizenship and full participation of all citizens was proclaimed with an ultimate goal of "the creation of a learning society committed to social justice and general well-being" (p. 1).

The *Declaration* contains a preamble of 27 statements and ten themes organized to provide a visionary framework for all UNESCO member states to "promote adult education as an integral part of a system of learning [and] ensure that lifelong learning will become a more significant reality in the early twenty-first century" (UNESCO, 1997, p. 1). However, it also recognized that these laudable goals faced many practical challenges and that profound changes were occurring, both globally and locally, that might affect their realization: economic globalization, deeply rooted problems of gender and racial inequity and oppression, rapid yet uneven development of science and technology, drastic demographic changes, the shift to a knowledge- and information-based society, intensifying crises in the environment, major changes in patterns of work and employment, and increasing tensions between social groups.

With the benefit of over 15 years of hindsight we note that, sadly, too many of these predictions have come to pass, and the worldwide appearance and expression of adult education and lifelong learning is now very different from those of 1997. Given the shifting nature of policy discourses and the challenges facing the international field of adult and continuing education (particularly as it tries to address the rapid changes in the social, economic, environmental, and political spheres), we feel it important to review critically the changes that have occurred in the intervening years and assess how far the visionary statements of the *Hamburg Declaration* have come to pass.

Of course, we are aware that others have explored similar concerns since the Hamburg conference. In 2003 the International Council for Adult Education undertook a systematic transnational review of progress towards the achievement of the various goals with data drawn from 16 countries in five continents (International Council for Adult Education, 2003). Later that same year, UNESCO's Institute for Education held a midterm review conference in Bangkok that brought together over three hundred representatives of 90+ member states (including ministers and senior-level officials), agencies of the United Nations system, nongovernmental and civil-society organizations, and academic and research institutions. The conference examined recent trends and new developments in practices and policies of adult learning and education and sought to align the CONFINTEA V agenda more closely with other UNESCO initiatives such as the Dakar Framework for Action and the United Nations Millennium Development Goals. Following the conference, a synthesis report was published that outlined the major issues and key recommendations and was designed to propose strategies for the advancement of adult learning to be followed in future programs (UNESCO, 2003). Then, in preparation for the 2009 CONFINTEA VI conference, UNESCO undertook a massive international study of adult education development among its member states. By the end of the survey period, 154 out of 195 countries had participated; based upon their responses, five regional synthesis reports were produced, along with the first-ever *Global Report on Adult Learning and Education* (GRALE; UNESCO Institute for Lifelong Learning, 2009). This report summarized recent trends, identified key challenges and best practices, and recommended courses of action to improve the worldwide scope of adult education and learning. As well, Forrester (1998), Preece (2011), and Schemmann (2007) have each published reflections on various aspects of CONFINTEA V and the *Hamburg Declaration* that, although more modest in scope, are no less insightful.

However, as important and astute as these documents are, none explicitly examines the *Hamburg Declaration* with a view to assessing how far adult education in general has responded to the political, social, economic, educational, and cultural transformations occurring globally. Indeed, given the recent challenges to peace and democracy throughout the world, we felt such a review of the *Hamburg Declaration*'s objectives and achievements is both necessary and timely. We are also aware that in many parts of the world, knowledge and appreciation of UNESCO's activities and approaches are not so strong as they might be. Consequently, we invited a range of North American and international scholars to review how the *Declaration*'s 10 themes had evolved since 1997, to determine their most recent local and global achievements through considering the results of the 2009 CONFINTEA VI conference in Belém and other recent developments, and to outline what still remains undone. Authors were chosen for their specific content expertise and their knowledge of, and commitment to, the broad educational goals of UNESCO.

We are also aware that the deliberations at international conferences often seem far removed from the day-to-day concerns of adult education practitioners. Yet, while we might (and do) bemoan the lack of involvement of adult educators and learners in policy forums, who can claim to know the issues better than those most closely involved? Ultimately, the decisions taken in conferences like CONFINTEA affect all who work in and study adult education. So, mindful of such issues, we were concerned that this volume should interest practitioners as well as scholars and policy makers. Thus we encouraged chapter authors to balance theory, research, and practice, and as far as possible to provide practical examples to illustrate their arguments and highlight exemplary instances of thematic achievement.

The volume closely follows the *Hamburg Declaration*'s 10 themes. In Chapter 1 Michael Welton sets the tone of the overall discussion by addressing Theme 1: "Adult learning and democracy: The challenges of the twenty-first century." He first considers the current (and often dramatic) demonstrations for greater democracy in several Arab countries and then the recent challenges to the established economic and political orders closer at hand. In each instance, adult education has played a significant part, and Welton explores its role in shaping and informing those events. In Chapter 2 Daniel Wagner explores Themes 2 and 3: "Improving the conditions and quality of adult learning" and "Ensuring the universal right to literacy and basic education." He reminds us that since its founding, UNESCO has always put literacy at the top of its education and human rights agenda and that now, more than six decades later, it still maintains its role at the forefront of global literacy efforts. In his chapter, Wagner describes how UNESCO has sought to accomplish this mission, explores the prospects for the future as the United Nations Literacy Decade draws to a close, and discusses some of the differences between OECD and UNESCO approaches to ALE.

In Chapter 3 Nelly P. Stromquist examines Theme 4: "Adult learning, gender equality and equity, and the empowerment of women." Considering Fraser's recognition and redistributive conceptualizations of gender, she examines the objectives of both CONFINTEA V and VI from a gender perspective. Next, she assesses the impact of the *Hamburg Declaration* and concludes by analyzing the likely path of future state action on adult education for women. In Chapter 4 Amy Rose explores Theme 5: "Adult learning and the changing world of work." She considers how increasing globalization has affected the nature of work and workplace relations and examines some of the trends indicated in the *Hamburg Declaration*. Next, she documents some examples of the ways workplace learning has incorporated these trends into learning situations and questions why the notion of innovation as the source of industrial growth was not considered in those parts of the *Declaration* that dealt with workplace commitments.

In Chapter 5 Darlene E. Clover and Robert Hill explore Theme 6: "Adult learning in relation to environment, health and population." They reflect on changing adult education approaches to environmental issues through an exploration of the main United Nations conferences on the environment and environmental education. They discuss the philosophical ideas captured in CONFINTEA V documents before moving to an analysis of the discussions at CONFINTEA VI. They conclude by focusing on some of the key directions in which environmental adult education and learning must head if the field is to support people's actions to contest and exercise power on the neoliberal ecological landscape. In Chapter 6 Dejan Dinevski and Marko Radovan look at Theme 7: "Adult learning, culture, media and new information technologies." They reflect on the possibilities contained in the *Hamburg Declaration*, explore the extent to which these optimistic objectives have been achieved, and then examine the challenges and possibilities of digital technologies in promoting access to adult learning and fostering interaction of adults with other cultures and society in general.

In Chapter 7 Alan Tuckett considers Themes 8 and 10: "Adult learning for all: The rights and aspirations of different groups" and "Enhancing international cooperation and solidarity." He examines the background to the Hamburg conference, and to the energy and confidence generated by the process that culminated in CONFINTEA V's *Hamburg Declaration*. He next discusses various developments since then, which have generally resulted in a diminution of opportunities for adult learning, particularly among the most disadvantaged groups. However, Tuckett counters this and provides some positive examples that show increased collaboration between some sectors that should be of benefit to all. In Chapter 8 Richard Desjardins explores Theme 9: "The economics of adult learning." He assesses the current world-wide state of financing adult learning and education and reviews how the issue of adult education funding has evolved over time. He assesses its most recent local and global achievements through a consideration of the results of the CONFINTEA VI conference and other recent developments, and outlines what still remains to be done.

Finally, in Chapter 9 Tom Nesbit summarizes the developments considered in the earlier chapters and assesses the extent to which, overall, the utopian aims of the *Hamburg Declaration* have been achieved. He explores several organizational and conceptual issues that have prevented the full realization of the *Declaration's* potential, lists some of the more positive changes that have taken place since 1997, and concludes with some suggestions about how the hope and promise of the *Hamburg Declaration* can be reaffirmed and reenergized.

Tom Nesbit
Michael Welton
Editors

References

Alfred, M. V., & Nafukho, F. M. (2010). International and comparative adult and continuing education. In C. E. Kasworm, A. D. Rose, & J. M. Ross-Gordon (Eds.), *Handbook of adult and continuing education* (pp. 93–102). Thousand Oaks, CA: Sage.

Delors, J. (1996). *Learning: The treasure within.* Report to UNESCO of the International Commission on Education for the Twenty-First Century. Paris, France: UNESCO.

Duke, C. (1994). Research in adult education: Current trends and future agenda. In W. Mauch (Ed.), *World trends in adult education research* (pp. 7–12). Hamburg, Germany: UNESCO Institute of Education.

Duke, C., & Hinzen, H. (2011). Adult education and lifelong learning within UNESCO: CONFINTEA, education for all, and beyond. *Adult Learning, 22*(4)–23(1), 18–23.

Faure, E. (1972). *Learning to be: The world of education today and tomorrow.* Paris, France: UNESCO.

Forrester, K. (1998). Adult learning: "A key for the twenty-first century": Reflections on the UNESCO fifth international conference. *International Journal of Lifelong Education, 17*(6), 423–434.

International Council for Adult Education. (2003). *Agenda for the future: Six years later.* Montevideo, Uruguay: Author.

Preece, J. (2011). Research in adult education and lifelong learning in the era of CONFINTEA VI. *International Journal of Lifelong Education, 30*(1), 99–117.

Rubenson, K. (2011). The field of adult education: An overview. In K. Rubenson (Ed.), *Adult education and learning* (pp. 3–13). Oxford, England: Elsevier.

Schemmann, M. (2007). CONFINTEA V from the world polity perspective. *Convergence, XL*(3–4), 157–168.

UNESCO. (1945). *Constitution.* Retrieved from http://portal.unesco.org/en/ev.php-URL _ID=15244&URL_DO=DO_TOPIC&URL_SECTION=201.html

UNESCO. (1976). *Recommendations on the development of adult education.* Paris, France: Author.

UNESCO. (1997). *The Hamburg Declaration on adult learning and agenda for the future*. Paris, France: Author.

UNESCO. (2003). *Recommitting to adult education and learning*. Paris, France: Author.

UNESCO Institute for Lifelong Learning. (2009). *Global report on adult learning and education*. Hamburg, Germany: Author.

TOM NESBIT *has recently retired from Simon Fraser University in Vancouver, BC, where he was associate dean of lifelong learning. He is a member of the educational sectoral council of the Canadian Commission for UNESCO.*

MICHAEL WELTON *is an adjunct professor with the Centre for Higher Education & Policy Studies at the University of British Columbia. He also tutors undergraduate courses in educational studies at Athabasca University.*

New Directions for Adult and Continuing Education • DOI: 10.1002/ace

1

This chapter addresses Theme 1 of the Hamburg Declaration: *Adult learning and democracy: The challenges of the twenty-first century.*

Subjects to Citizens: Adult Learning and the Challenges of Democracy in the Twenty-First Century

Michael Welton

Theme 1 of the *Hamburg Declaration on Adult Learning* boldly proclaimed that active citizenship and full participation of all citizens was the necessary foundation for "the creation of a learning society committed to social justice and general well-being" (UNESCO, 1997, p. 4). The *Declaration* advocated that future societies create "greater community participation"; raise "awareness about prejudice and discrimination in society"; encourage "greater recognition, participation and accountability of non-government organizations and local community groups"; and promote "a culture of peace, intercultural dialogue and human rights" (pp. 11–13). The comparative document from the most recent CONFINTEA VI conference—the *Belém Framework for Action* (UNESCO Institute for Lifelong Learning, 2009)—while committing itself to creating mechanisms for civil society involvement in decision-making, has muted and toned down the boldness of the earlier Declaration. Indeed, one can detect considerable hesitancy regarding active, engaged citizenry in language such as "constructive and informed involvement" and engagement where "appropriate."

This chapter will accent the *Hamburg Declaration's* prominent emphasis on promoting active citizenship through a vitalized civil society and open public spheres through examining two recent examples. Both the Arab Spring and the Occupy Movement provide a window to examine the state of participative democracy in 2012 and reveal a deep-seated aspiration to "become more involved in public decisions, through various practices and instruments that will make them more mature players, better able to cooperate with one

NEW DIRECTIONS FOR ADULT AND CONTINUING EDUCATION, no. 138, Summer 2013 © 2013 Wiley Periodicals, Inc.
Published online in Wiley Online Library (wileyonlinelibrary.com) • DOI: 10.1002/ace.20049

another" (Allegretti, 2012, p. iv). In the Middle East uprisings, one of the modes of participative democracy—"participation by storm" (protests and occupation) has taken precedence over "participation by invitation" (venues where citizens are "given the right" to express their views; Ibarra & Ahedo, 2007, p. iv). Challard (2011) observes pointedly that the flow of people pouring into the Middle Eastern streets was not influenced by a "single dime of aid earmarked for democracy" (p. 6). He maintains that Western aid is mostly for the military and that professionalized forms of activism reduced "civil society to the realm of bureaucratic NGOs and formalized 'grassroots' institutions" (p. 6). Thus, public spheres had to be created through civil disobedience. This latter form of learning and struggle is seldom mentioned in UNESCO policy documents. In fact, the gap between policy statements and decision-making processes ought to provoke adult educators to consider how they might nurture the moral and ethical motivation to act justly in an evil and degraded world.

The *Hamburg Declaration* centered around two key concepts: *globalization* and *civil society*. Prior to 1997, globalization had received little attention in UNESCO conferences. However, CONFINTEA V recognized that something new and disturbing was beginning to appear in the world's economic order: "True economic globalisation invokes a qualitative shift toward a global economic system that is no longer based on autonomous national economies but on a consolidated global marketplace for production, distribution and consumption" (Korsgaard, 1997, p. 11). The second key concept introduced at the Hamburg conference was civil society. The term carried hopefulness: no matter how oppressive the state might appear, citizens could communicate their ideas of a different world through underground writings, clandestine meetings in living rooms, and coalesce into a disruptive force at the right moment. Those interested in social learning theory worked hard to understand the nature of a legally constituted civil society and the role of social movements, civil disobedience, and public spheres in enabling citizens to acquire voice to articulate their needs and press these demands through the gateway into state decision-making.

Adult educators discussing these concepts at CONFINTEA V could not have imagined what the following 15 years would be like for participative democracy. They probably expected the neoliberal global economy named in the 1990s to chug along with periodic awful crises. But no one expected the world to be teetering on the edge of the destruction of the "institutional framework of globalization and undermining of the post-1989 international order" (Davis, 2011, p. 6). Or imagine that the new century would begin with the crashing of hijacked jets into the World Trade Center, the Pentagon, and a field in Pennsylvania by terrorists acting in the name of Islam or that Bin Laden and Al-Qaeda would become familiar names throughout the world.

Then, quickly following the horrific events of 9/11, the United States and its allies invaded Iraq and Afghanistan. The invasion of two Islamic countries corroded the spirit of democracy: the U.S. government thought it could impose "democracy" on the countries they had invaded and forced a national-security regime on their own citizens. Most significantly, 9/11 cast its very dark shadow over the entire decade. The "war on terror" shaped its mood—morose and melancholic. In academic circles, a veritable revolution occurred—suddenly the old secularization thesis of the 1980s and 1990s collapsed. Religion could hardly be understood to be a private affair anymore. Stunned academics shook off the dust and began to rethink revered assumptions about the role that religion was really playing in the entire world—Muslim worlds, Africa, Latin America, the United States, and not just "exceptional Europe" with its beautiful and empty churches. Those framing the *Hamburg Declaration*—calling for the building of cultures of peace and intercultural dialogue and respect—had their hopes dashed as religious intolerance intensified through the decade, culminating recently in September, 2012 in worldwide Islamic violent reaction to the crudely made anti-Islam video by American right-wing extremists. Today, a burgeoning literature (for example, Butler, Habermas, Taylor, & West, 2011; Habermas, 2002; Habermas, Brieskorn, Peder, Ricker, & Schmidt, 2010) argues that participative democracy (the form with greatest affinity to adult education thought) is inconceivable without religious and secular persons accepting each other as equals in public debate and consideration. A "culture of peace" requires that this happen. And adult educators everywhere must institute social practices and design pedagogical instruments to reconcile those engaged in sectarian conflict and violence.

For a society to be authentically democratic, its civil society and public spheres must be legally constituted. The rights of freedom of speech and assembly must be entitlements of the citizenry. Voluntary associations, social movements, and public spheres must be permitted, and the right to protest civilly against various government policies must be in place. The military must be under the rule of law. Those who govern must be accountable for their actions. If these roughly set out criteria are taken as benchmarks, then any scan of the world would reveal that very few societies are democracies. Even the liberal democratic countries now in the grip of neoliberal ideas and practices have made it extremely difficult for a normally functioning civil society to have much influence over government policies. The chasm between civil society and the state in liberal democratic countries has grown very wide between 1997 and 2012. The gateways or sluices from civil society to the state (or the reverse) have either collapsed or been left in tatters.

For Elizabeth Anderson (2011), "The attacks [on the World Trade Center and Pentagon] were used to rationalize a massive expansion of the national security state, an unwarranted war in in Iraq, a quagmire in Afghanistan, torture and abuse of prisoners, extraordinary rendition of terrorism suspects, indefinite detention of prisoners at Guantanamo Bay, and the use of cluster bombs and drone attacks that has resulted in massive civil casualties" (p. 23). She thinks that the corrosion of democratic spirit has continued by the failure to close Guantanamo Bay, shift terrorism trials to civil courts or even prosecute government officials who ordered torture. The warfare state is growing, not receding. Habermas (2006) agrees: "In the United States itself, the administration of a perpetual 'wartime president' is already undermining the foundations of the rule of law" (2006, p. 34). Like other American critical scholars, Anderson (2011) believes that

> The central institutions Americans count on to check abuses of state power— laws promoting transparency in government, a vigorous, skeptical press; competitive press; competitive political parties; an independent judiciary empowered to enforce constitutional rights failed to check the political dynamics of fear-mongering. (p. 24)

The mighty republic has become the "Quiet Republic"—there is hardly any public deliberation on these serious matters.

Arab Spring

History is full of surprising moments when *revolutionary possibility* breaks through cement roadways and radical new directions (or *political imaginaries*) are opened up. Before animosity to *political Islamists* willing to harness terror to "religion" had died down, the unthinkable occurred in the Middle East. In early December 2010, Mohamed Bouazzi, a Tunisian university graduate who had failed to gain a permit to sell his vegetables and fruit, dowsed himself with fuel and set himself ablaze. This very ordinary moment of everyday life (facing the tangle of bureaucracy) transformed into something extraordinary. Bouazzi became a potent symbol of the humiliations, indignities, and oppression suffered by millions living in authoritarian dictatorships in the Middle East (and elsewhere, too). In January 2011, hundreds of thousands of protesters, mostly young, poured into the streets to attempt to topple their dictatorial regimes. Within months, Ben Ali of Tunisia and Hosni Mubarak of Egypt were gone. In the springtime euphoria, Mustafa Barghouti (2011), head of the Palestinian Medical Relief Committee, wrote that the "revolutionary tidal wave, which began in Tunisia and Algeria, reached its crest in Egypt and is currently sweeping other countries such as Libya and Bahrain" (p. 1). He thought that "great revolutions cannot be made. They erupt, like volcanos, atop of the mounting force of huge and long-suppressed social and political contradictions" (p. 1).

Those who study the Arab world know well the roots of Arab unrest and the various historic struggles for constitutional democracy in its past. The Cairo Institute for Human Rights Studies (CIHRS) has published reports that document a litany of disturbing abuses that have characterized 12 countries in the Arab world (Egypt, Tunisia, Algeria, Morocco, Iraq, Syria, Lebanon, Yemen, Bahrain, Saudi Arabia, Sudan, and the occupied Palestinian territories). Its most recent report (CIHRS, 2012b) cites the deteriorating state of human rights, the lack of political will to advance human rights, stagnant legislatures, perpetuation of authoritarian approaches to entrenching impunity for gross violations, state of emergency used to justify serious crimes (such as extrajudicial killings, abductions, and involuntary disappearances), continuing policies that cement and perpetuate rule or hereditary succession, falsification of citizens' will through rigged general elections, and the blocking of freedom of expression.

A revolutionary moment opens the world's window, drawing people into a social learning process that can awaken them to see with new eyes. Arab people have been suffering, suffocating, and struggling under authoritarian rulers forever. For example, Palestinians continue to be the targets of egregious abuse by Israel, Yemenis were encountering social and political unrest before the people took to the streets and faced machine guns, Egypt has been in a "state of emergency" since the early 1990s, Syria has a nasty history of destroying any political opposition, Saudi Arabia represses religious freedoms and its Shiite minority faces systematic discrimination, and the Bashir regime in the Sudan commits war crimes in Darfur. Against this ghastly backdrop, the Arab Spring cracked through the fear in the name of human dignity and freedom and justice. It might be called the "dignity revolution": millions of Arabs had experienced the indignities of neoliberalism and decades of repression (CIHRS, 2012b). Then the dam burst.

The revolution was, in fact, partly about bread (in Egypt the cost had risen astronomically) and partly about the arising of a "younger generation of activists, both in the West and in the Arab world, [who] was increasingly asserting itself and forging a more nuanced discourse" (LeVine, 2012, p. 2). The young activists whose faces were observed in Tahrir Square had moved beyond those old Nasserite, hard left, or Islamists who had focused their attention on the role of Western imperialism in the plight of the Arab world. They were right to do so: the West—as was revealed brazenly in the Arab Spring uprisings—supported the dictatorships because they preferred stability and not democracy. But by 2006, the young activists were calling for a new Arab movement for change (LeVine, 2012). They wanted to focus on protecting their own fragile civil societies against repressive governments. At this time, Internet-friendly grassroots movements such as *Kefaya* were a crucible for creating new forms of action and discourse that would help launch the January 25 revolution.

Egypt's neoliberal policies had triggered revolts in industrial cities such as Mahallah in 2006 and 2008, as well as in Gafasa, Tunisia in 2008. Militant labor activists—who had a long history of anti-government resistance—joined with the "cyber-generation of civil society activists to form movements such as April 6, and together would provide the nucleus of the 'movement of movements' that would form the revolutionary coalition of late 2010 and 2011" (LeVine, 2012, p. 3). The financial crisis of 2008 legitimated anti-neoliberal movements in Europe and North America. The intensity and depth of the crisis in the Arab world, linked with its history of authoritarian regimes, sparked the revolt. Thus, we can understand the Arab revolution through using creatively the two concepts of globalization and civil society apparent in the *Hamburg Declaration*.

Now, almost two years after the January revolutions in Egypt and Tunisia (with fighting and mayhem still continuing in Syria, Yemen, and elsewhere), the balloon full of revolutionary hopes and dreams has lost air and returned to Earth with questionable gains:

> Over the past three years, the Arab and Muslim world—from Morocco to Iran, from Syria to Yemen—seems to have witnessed more mass demonstrations than in the entire history of all postcolonial nation-states combined. Where do Iranians and Arabs—and, by extension, the rest of the Muslim world—stand today after shedding their fear of brutality, risking everything for a better, yet uncertain, future for themselves and their children? (Dabashi, 2012, p. 1)

This question is stirring up a mighty storm of debate throughout the Middle East and beyond. The CIHRS fourth annual report (2012a), which analyzes the state of human rights in 2011 in the 12 previously named Arab countries, points out:

> It is clear that the achievements of the Arab uprisings have not equaled the sacrifices made by the peoples who rebelled in search of freedom, social justice, and human dignity. With the exception of Tunisia, the choices facing these peoples seem limited to narrow reform of old regimes or the hegemony of Islamist factions over the institutions of governance and the erosion of the foundations of the civil state. (para. 1)

The people have removed the symbols of tyranny in Tunisia, Egypt, Libya, and Yemen. That is only the initial "disclosing of a new sense of solidarity and a reinvigorated notion of citizenship" (Challard, 2011).

The Egyptian case illustrates some hard truths about making a revolution. Revolutions are not made on Facebook or in cyberspace but through hard and long organizing on the ground, face to face. Perhaps some of the youth and others who made the revolution, gathering repeatedly in Tahrir Square, were naïve to think that the old regime (led by the Supreme Council of the Armed Forces [SCAF]) would just fade away. It didn't: the revolutionaries could not agree on a new constitution. They thought they could remove Mubarak without changing the regime, they did not provide a "unified front" to the old regime (they fragmented and splintered into Islamists, nationalists, liberals, and leftists), and the Muslim Brotherhood got greedy and tried to dominate the legislature. This provided SCAF the opportunity to "recover its force, unify its assets and move centre-stage once again" (Bishara, 2012, p. 1). These events happened through the summer and early fall.

As I write this chapter in mid-December 2012, Morsi has trumped SCAF and declared himself above the law and offered a contentious draft constitution to the Egyptian people for voting. Egypt is undergoing a trying and difficult post-revolutionary learning process. Once again Tahrir Square is filled with tumultuous and edgy demonstrations—roughly dividing into the Muslim Brotherhood supporters on one side and leftists, secularists, and liberals on the other. After 60 years of singular rule, Egyptians are learning to disagree. Larbi Sadiki (2012), professor of Middle East Studies at the University of Exeter, counsels us to see that the

> cries of freedom and dignity should not be orientalised into inhospitality to democracy, as many argue today. Rather, every riot, every protest, and every demonstration manifests forms of horizontal politics without which resistance and interrogation of old hierarchies and attendant power relations cannot be enacted. (p. 1)

Many voices are crisscrossing in the public square as Egyptians learn how to dialogue and compromise without excluding the other. Egyptians are struggling over the appropriate constitutional form that recognizes historic traditions and caters to all in society. They are also battling over the role of the courts and their legal system. They are also grappling intensely with the role that religion should play in Egyptian society. As we glance backward to remember the violence and bloodshed attending the historic struggles for democracy in France and the United States, we are reminded that constructing the appropriate vertical and horizontal institutions and learning processes is extremely challenging (in the Middle East and everywhere else).

The Occupy Movement

2011 may go down in history as the "year of occupations." In May, Spaniards filled the square at Puerto de Sol in Madrid. Initiated by the *Real Democracy Now* organization, the indignados protested against their inegalitarian economic system, a democracy that no longer represented them and the evident "financial coup" that simply placed unelected men from the financial sector into important positions. The occupation of the Puerto de Sol Square lasted a month. Adult education in the form of general assemblies, discussions, and working groups attracted thousands of people. After the initial gatherings, the movement named itself 15-M. A nonpartisan social movement, 15-M catalyzed significant public debate through setting up assemblies in various neighborhoods and presented a flood of proposals to engage the public in the Spanish election. Influenced by the Arab Spring (if they can do it, why not us?), the 15-M movement in turn inspired the Chilean students to take to the streets to protest their government's neoliberal policies of privatized public education: one more expensive commodity. The Chilean student movement "staged some of the biggest popular demonstrations since Chile returned to democracy; it spread to families and high schools and raised questions about inequalities and tax reform as well as representation in the political system" (Kempf, 2012, p. 14).

Kempf (2012) perceptively observes "that feeling of unease about a political system slipping from the control of citizens, and even more of wealth being monopolized by an oligarchy, provoked the launching of the Occupy Movement, with Occupy Wall Street (OWS) in New York on 17 September" (p. 14). Several hundred people gathered in Manhattan's financial district and found themselves near Zuccotti Park, a small square surrounded by towering skyscrapers, close to Ground Zero. Someone suggested that a general assembly be held there—as in Greece and Spain. Rare for the United States, Americans began conversations about politics on the streets and in public spaces. The OWS movement grew—with more general assemblies and working groups—these ragged kinds of collective learning processes are difficult to assess. At the base of the occupation movements is the powerful idea that actually occupying public space is the fundamental way to be heard. That was enough for some; others were pressed to think of other forms of action (particularly when the police used violence to rid Zuccotti Park of its residents).

Kempf (2012) acknowledges the diversity of initiatives and ideas in OWS and documents other outcomes—such as "Occupy Our Homes," a "US-wide event to reclaim empty houses that had been foreclosed by banks" (p. 14). But he correctly claims that "inequalities and the crisis of representation in the political system" lay beneath these protests and that OWS was a "'movement of movements,' able to draw attention to other campaigns that would not have had as much impact without OWS support" (p. 15). The Occupy Movement spread to many cities in Canada, the United States, and Europe: Occupy London, camped around St. Paul's Cathedral, targeted the London Stock Exchange. Now Egyptian activists could text their American, European, or Canadian comrades on their streets, developing new forms of cosmopolitan solidarity.

Conclusion

Since Hamburg 1997, we have witnessed startling, distressing, exhilarating, and modestly hopeful events. Globalization (in its neoliberal form) and the endless humiliations of tyrannical dictatorships intersected at (impossible to predict) "revolutionary moments" unleashing an intense social learning process that manifested in collective action in the massive gatherings in various public squares in the Middle East. These public spaces precipitated complex forms of consciousness-raising and steeled the courage of those facing armies, thugs, and police. The reaction of the regimes to the collective protests led, in turn, to deepened understandings of the nature of the regime and what they had to take into account to change the regimes. As the Egyptian case illustrates, the question of how the transition to authentic, constitutionally grounded new societies occurs has not yet crystallized.

This brief analysis of the Arab Spring and the Occupy Movement indicates that we are living in a time of disorder, mayhem, and instability. The regimes in the Middle East are still in a process of becoming, and it is not clear whether they will take on a participative shape. The United States does not have control over what is happening. It prefers stable dictatorships and not authentic democracies. The U.S.–Israeli threat to bomb Iran's alleged nuclear bomb–producing facilities shadows the Middle East as does the sectarian war in Syria (with the great powers divided over support for the present regime). And the role of Islamist political movements in the uprisings (and non-Islamic forms of extremism in other settings) threatens orderly unfolding to a secular state respecting all religious and secular orientations. But there will be no return to the status quo ante: a new imaginary has broken into the Middle East and, we dare think, into the rest of the world as well. Canadian scholars Jocelyn Maclure and Charles Taylor (2011) argue that we must "learn to coexist and, ideally, to establish bonds of solidarity. We believe in an ethics of dialogue respectful of the different moral and spiritual options." This disposition is "best able to promote that learning process" (p. 110).

References

Allegretti, G. (2012). Participate, but how? *Le Monde Diplomatique* [Supplement], September, iv.

Anderson, E. (2011). The war at home. *Democracy, 22*, 23–25.

Barghouti, M. (2011). *Lessons from the Egyptian revolution.* Retrieved from http://weekly.ahram.org.eg/print/2011/1037/op181.htm

Bishara, M. (2012). *What went wrong in Egypt?* Retrieved from http://www.aljazeera.com/indepth/opinion/2012/06/20126178810737689.html

Butler, J., Habermas, J., Taylor, C., & West, C. (2011). *The power of religion in the public sphere.* New York, NY: Columbia University Press.

Cairo Institute for Human Rights Studies. (2012a). *Dilemma of the "Arab Spring": Inadequate reforms, erosion of the civil state, denial of justice.* Retrieved from http://www.cihrs.org/?p=2591&lang=en

Cairo Institute for Human Rights Studies. (2012b). *2009 report on human rights in the Arab world: Bastion of impunity, mirage of reform.* Press release. Retrieved from http://www.cihrs.org/?p=1119&lang=en

Challard, B. (2011). The counter-power of civil society and the emergence of a new political imaginary in the Arab world. *Constellations, 18.* doi:10.1111/j.1467-8675.2011.0065

Dabashi, H. (2012). *Revolution: The pursuit of public happiness.* Retrieved from http://www.aljazeera.com/indepth/opinion/2012/06/2012618759252770.html

Davis, M. (2011). Spring confronts winter. *New Left Review, 72*(November–December), 5–15.

Habermas, J. (2002). *Religion and rationality: Essays on reason, God, and modernity.* Cambridge, MA: MIT Press.

Habermas, J. (2006). *The divided West.* Cambridge, England: Polity Press.

Habermas, J., Brieskorn, N., Peder, M., Ricker, F., & Schmidt, J. (2010). *An awareness of what is missing: Faith and reason in a post-secular age.* Cambridge, England: Polity Press.

Ibarra, P., & Ahedo, I. (2007). *Democracia participative y desarrollo humano [Democratic participation and human development].* Madrid, Spain: Dykinson.

Kempf, R. (2012). The year of occupation. *Le Monde Diplomatique, 1205*(May), 14–15.

Korsgaard, O. (Ed.). (1997). *Adult learning and the challenges of the 21st century*. Odense, Denmark: Association for World Education.

LeVine, M. (2012). *From 9/11 to 2/11: How Egypt's revolution became the world's*. Retrieved from http://aljazeera.com/indepth/opinion/2012/02 /2012211113047986549.html

Maclure, J., & Taylor, C. (2011). *Secularism and freedom of conscience*. Cambridge, MA: Harvard University Press.

Sadiki, L. (2012). *The Arab Spring: Disorder may be good?* Retrieved from http://aljazeera .com/indepth/opinion/2012/12/20121212148394704.html

UNESCO. (1997). *The Hamburg Declaration on adult learning and agenda for the future*. Paris, France: Author.

UNESCO Institute for Lifelong Learning. (2009). *Harnessing the power and potential of adult learning and education for a viable future: Belém framework for action*. Hamburg, Germany: Author.

MICHAEL WELTON *is an adjunct professor with the Centre for Higher Education & Policy Studies at the University of British Columbia. He also tutors undergraduate courses in educational studies at Athabasca University.*

2

This chapter addresses Themes 2 & 3 of the Hamburg Declaration: *Improving the conditions and quality of adult learning and Ensuring the universal right to literacy and basic education.*

Literacy and UNESCO: Conceptual and Historical Perspectives*

Daniel Wagner

At its founding in 1946, UNESCO put literacy at the top of its education and human rights agenda. More than six decades later, UNESCO maintains (on its website) the mission statement: "UNESCO is at the forefront of global literacy efforts and is dedicated to keeping literacy high on national, regional and international agendas." This chapter briefly describes how UNESCO has sought to accomplish this mission and its prospects for the future. With its claimed status as the leader in international literacy work, what UNESCO does, and does not, achieve will no doubt have an important impact on the future of literacy, especially in the low-income regions of the world that depend on external funding and technical assistance.

Literacy and UNESCO, 1946–2000

As part of the Universal Declaration of Human Rights in 1946, UNESCO put literacy at the top of its education mission. In the decades that followed, the United Nations and UNESCO reiterated support for literacy in the 1975 Persepolis Declaration, stating that: "Literacy is not an end in itself. It is a fundamental human right" (UNESCO, 1975; cited in UNESCO, 2005, p. 136); and the 1990 World Declaration on Education for All (EFA) declared that "literacy, oral expression, numeracy, and problem solving as essential learning

*This paper was originally presented in the panel: "Re-Imagining UNESCO: Past, Present and Future" at the Annual Meeting of the Comparative and International Education Society (Chicago, Illinois, March 4, 2010). Parts of the paper were also adapted from Wagner (2011).

NEW DIRECTIONS FOR ADULT AND CONTINUING EDUCATION, no. 138, Summer 2013 © 2013 Wiley Periodicals, Inc.
Published online in Wiley Online Library (wileyonlinelibrary.com) • DOI: 10.1002/ace.20050

tools that comprise the basic learning needs of every person . . . child, youth and adult" (UNESCO, 1990, p. 6).

Later, the 1997 *Hamburg Declaration on Adult Learning* stated under Resolution 11 that "literacy, broadly conceived as the basic knowledge and skills needed by all in a rapidly changing world, is a fundamental human right" (UNESCO, 1997, p. 4). Over its first 54 years, UNESCO affirmed and reaffirmed its leadership role in the "battle for literacy." Over the years, UNESCO focused mainly on nonformal education programs for adults (and out-of-school youth)—what was broadly termed adult learning. Operationally, and in terms of visibility, UNESCO made one of its first major technical impacts by responding to an increasing demand for comparative data on literacy. By the mid-1950s and in the decades that followed, UNESCO produced a wide variety of empirical reports on adult literacy rates, and these data formed the basis for other UN and bilateral agencies to report literacy levels and consider regional and national literacy priorities, especially in developing countries. To obtain its data, UNESCO initially depended on national education authorities to provide statistics on basic education and literacy, most of which were derived from school or program attendance records.

The first major UNESCO international report on literacy in UNESCO (1978) was based on the following: "In the projection exercise, school enrolment ratios for the 6–11 age group were utilized for estimating future illiteracy rates for the 15–19 age group, and these in turn, together with the United Nations demographic projections, were then utilized for estimating future illiteracy rates for the population aged 15 and over" (Smyth, 2005, p. 12). Language of assessment and language of instruction clearly play a major role in determining not only the status of national literacy rates, but also the success of implementation (Robinson, 2005); these constraints in data collection have made both policy and implementation more difficult.

In the 1980s, the UN statistical office began to commission household surveys of adult literacy that used direct skill measurement (Wagner & Srivastava, 1989). By the 1990s, national governments (Canada and the United States, as well as the OECD), began a series of adult literacy surveys that started to replace UNESCO's data in industrialized countries. This was primarily due to increased sophistication of direct measurement of skills, an approach that was designed to help move beyond UNESCO's dependence on national estimates of literacy levels (Wagner, 1990). During this same period, the use of literacy statistics as part of the Human Development Index by UNDP, and as part of UNICEF and World Bank development reports, put increasing pressure on UNESCO to provide reliable and comparable data on literacy, but little in the way of fiscal means was provided to do more than urge better approaches on its member states.

During UNESCO's first half-century, there were also changes in the way it, and others, viewed literacy. These changes encompassed how literacy was defined—for example, as a cognitive and measurable skill (or skills) versus ways of "understanding the world" (as in Paulo Freire's work on empowerment).

During these years, UNESCO often found itself adopting the exhortatory approach of illiteracy "eradication" (treating illiteracy as a disease), the "battle" against illiteracy, and the comparison of literacy to a "light bulb," in that a person is in the dark until liberated into the "light" of literacy. These meta-phorical, rhetorical exhortations to literacy were not, however, the only way that literacy was promoted in UNESCO. During the 1960s, UNESCO (in part-nership with UNDP) sponsored the Experimental World Literacy Program, which sought to foster "functional literacy," tied to jobs and economic growth (UNESCO/UNDP, 1976). The 1990 EFA Conference concentrated on primary schooling, and for the first time focused major attention on the quality of learning in the classroom, a topic that would wait nearly two more decades before it would become a central UNESCO educational concern. Yet 1990 was also the UN International Literacy Year, during which some progress was made in rethinking how UNESCO was going to foster literacy in developing countries (Wagner, 1992).

The first half-century of effort by UNESCO to keep adult literacy (and adult learning more generally) in the spotlight can be seen as a cup either half-empty or half-full. On the one hand, UNESCO was practically the only inter-national agency championing literacy, at a time when other agencies were focused much more on other dimensions of the international education enterprise—for example, UNICEF on young children and primary schooling, and the World Bank on the formal school system and higher education. With respect to the World Bank, Jones (1997) emphasized its insistence on a human capital approach, tied to formal education and the global economy. Literacy—especially adult literacy and adult learning—was seen as too political and insufficiently linked to direct economic development. Jones summed up World Bank specialists' hesitancy on literacy as follows: "The answer might rather lie in Bank preference for schooling and learning systems which are easily controlled and managed, easily integrated with the formation of a citi-zenry and workforce unlikely to upset any political or cultural apple carts" (p. 374). Only UNESCO kept a spotlight on literacy, but the intensity of its beam was limited by constraints on human and fiscal resources, and an uncer-tain uptake on new methods and concepts for literacy statistics and innova-tion. Further, UNESCO was constantly buffeted by its member states, which pushed many education issues, not just literacy.

Literacy and UNESCO, 2000–2010

In 2000, UNESCO and other agencies organized a second Education for All (EFA) conference in Dakar (Senegal), during which 164 countries agreed to the Dakar Framework for Action, including the goal to increase literacy levels worldwide by 50% in the year 2015. This was also the occasion to take a new look at a number of key issues in literacy work, from definitions and measure-ment to the role of mother-tongue education, the relationship between child and adult literacy, and new conceptualizations of literacy based on cultural variation (Wagner, 2000). Several years later, when the United States (and some other nations) decided to rejoin UNESCO as member states, the United Nations Literacy Decade (UNLD; 2003–2012) was launched. The UNLD mandate would focus on "literacy for all [since it] is at the heart of basic education for all . . . [and] creating literate environments and societies is essential for achieving the goals of eradicating poverty, reducing child mortality, curbing population growth, achieving gender equality and ensuring sustainable development, peace and democracy" (United Nations, 2002; cited in UNESCO, 2005, p. 31). As part of the Decade, the UNESCO Institute for Lifelong Learning (UIL) led a program called Literacy for Empowerment (LIFE), which sponsored a number of regional literacy activities, and has tried to serve as a "catalyst for planning, capacity development, partnership building" (UNESCO Institute for Lifelong Learning, 2009, p. 13).

Four major activities during this decade merit further comment. The first is the comprehensive 2006 Global Monitoring Report (GMR) entitled *Literacy for life* (UNESCO, 2005). This comprehensive review covered the major issues in literacy as understood by the best specialists in the world and also raised many questions that have troubled the literacy field since the beginning of UNESCO—including, for example, definitions of literacy, current statistics (and their problems), and innovative ideas for moving the field forward.

A second notable activity is the Literacy Assessment and Monitoring Program (LAMP), which was designed to build on previous international assessment efforts and has coincided with the current growth in international educational assessments. LAMP is undertaken by the UNESCO Institute for Statistics (UIS) and has based its approach methodologically on the earlier work of the OECD in the IALS international survey (OECD, 2000). According to the UIS, "the ultimate goal of LAMP is not to produce an international report and an international dataset to be used for research purposes but to contribute to the development of national capacities" (UNESCO Institute for Statistics, 2009, p. 24). A recent evaluation of LAMP, commissioned by the UIS, noted the unusually long time taken for delivery of implementation (from its inception in 2003 to 2008, only pilot work was achieved). In terms of implementation issues, this evaluation recommended that "within country priorities may require development of tests and instruments that are culture specific, whereas cross-country comparability priorities require tests and instruments to be culture-free so that they may be used appropriately in all of the participating countries" (Ercikan, Arim, Oliveri, & Sandilands, 2008, p. 5).

Third, the CONFINTEA VI conference in Belèm reaffirmed the importance of adult learning (and literacy) for the 21st century (UNESCO, 2010). The *Belém Framework* lays out the importance of adult literacy:

> Literacy is an indispensable foundation that enables young people and adults to engage in learning opportunities at all stages of the learning continuum. The right to literacy is an inherent part of the right to education. It is a prerequisite for the

development of personal, social, economic and political empowerment. Literacy is an essential means of building people's capabilities to cope with the evolving challenges and complexities of life, culture, economy and society. (p. 38)

This is very similar to the *Hamburg Declaration*'s definition of literacy:

> The basic knowledge and skills needed by all in a rapidly changing world, is a fundamental human right. In every society literacy is a necessary skill in itself and one of the foundations of other life skills. … Literacy is also a catalyst for participation in social, cultural, political and economic activities, and for learning throughout life. (p. 4)

Though one could argue that there are few differences between the Hamburg and Belém final proclamations, a greater emphasis on the measurement (monitoring, evaluation, and assessment) of adult learning and literacy seems evident in the Belém document.

Fourth, UNESCO published the 2010 Global Monitoring Report (GMR), *Reaching the Marginalized*. Although it focused on how to address the challenges of those individuals at greatest risk of not receiving an adequate education, this GMR also paid special attention to problems of illiteracy and low literacy among ethno-linguistic minority groups. Indeed, the 2010 GMR broke new ground by its recognition that national literacy statistics (along with other educational statistics) often missed those most in need as a result of restricted data collection methods and concepts that systematically excluded marginalized populations. Hopefully, this message will receive increased attention by the literacy community in the coming years.

UNESCO's literacy work is probably best known through the statistics that it has been providing on global literacy for a half-century, which are widely cited by other UN agencies as well as the media. As is well known, UNESCO was designed to serve member states. Yet UNESCO also tries to be a leader in developing ideas and improving technical competence in key areas such as literacy and adult learning. Thus, UNESCO serves a much larger world of constituents than just its member states when it publishes its reports and empirical findings. Even so, the statistics provided by UNESCO (now largely through the UIS in Montreal) are based today largely on the same methodology (national government estimations, mainly on schooling or indirect self-assessment surveys), and therefore suffer from the same lack of credibility (at least among experts) that has been the case over the years. This is one reason for the success of the OECD and other agencies taking a leadership role in literacy assessment in adults and in schools (most notably through the Program for International Student Assessment [PISA] and the Program for the International Assessment of Adult Competencies [PIAAC]). Some argue that UNESCO cannot do everything and that its resources are limited. But the main problem seems not that other agencies are implementing more credible and sound assessment data; rather, it is that UNESCO continues to publish comparative statistics that few experts take seriously as reliable data.

The difficulty of UNESCO to readjust or recalibrate its work towards accepted professional practice on literacy measurement is a matter of substantive concern, and a reflection on the limits of scientific professional capacity that have troubled UNESCO's work. On the other hand, as Smyth (2005) credibly noted regarding UNESCO's literacy statistics, UNESCO professionals were not unaware of the criticism of its data gathering. Rather, they simply had to balance both the multiple needs of nations and cultural perspectives, as well as the difficulty of focusing on both national and international policy needs. It has been argued that some of these limitations are due at least in part to UNESCO's reorganization in 2006—a change that effectively reduced political support and personnel in literacy in UNESCO Headquarters in Paris (Limage, 2007, 2009). In addition, one could also argue that other international stakeholders (such as the World Bank and major bilateral donors) tended to push their own educational and statistical agendas, to the detriment of UNESCO's. This may be reflected in the United Nations MDGs, which do not mention literacy as a focus of any of the eight goals.

Taken as a whole, UNESCO's literacy efforts in the past decade have seen some solid gains, particularly in a greater opening to new ideas as well as in the area of producing highly respected GMRs that have advanced thinking on literacy and related areas. At the same time, promises for improved and credible literacy statistics, the improved science of literacy development, and innovative ways to implement literacy programs have remained elusive.

UNESCO's Future in Literacy

Looking back on UNESCO's more than 60 years of work on literacy and adult learning, there is little question that it has been a major player and has kept itself at the forefront of policy debates and agendas. However, the more difficult question is whether it has been able to play a true leadership role—in the sense of accomplishments, providing conceptual guidance, and innovation—in improving literacy throughout this same period. It is easy to state that considerable educational progress has been made over the past half-century, but nearly all of this seems to have been achieved through the expansion of access to primary schooling across the globe, rather than through literacy and adult learning programs per se. Further, levels of low literacy and illiteracy remain a significant problem in the 21st century, especially in developing countries, and there has been only modest implementation engagement by UNESCO (UNESCO, 2005). In the area of adult literacy, when considered in light of the larger community of actors (governmental, nongovernmental, donor, etc.), UNESCO, even as an acknowledged institutional leader, is commonly perceived as an underachiever in terms of inputs, outputs, or innovative research and development. Indeed, as UNESCO itself has stated recently: "Literacy remains among the most neglected of all education goals. Progress towards the 2015 target of halving illiteracy [EFA Goal 4] has been far too slow and uneven" (2010, p. 94). As noted, it may have suited other international agencies to leave UNESCO with what may be termed as an "unfunded mandate" in literacy; these other agencies invested substantial resources in more attractive and tractable areas, such as primary and secondary schooling.

What should the field of literacy and adult learning expect from UNESCO over the next decade? If it desires to achieve its self-stated mission to be at "the forefront of global literacy efforts and . . . dedicated to keeping literacy high on national, regional and international agendas," then UNESCO will likely be able to meet this restricted goal, mainly because few other major institutional actors would wish to assume it. On the other hand, as literacy is at the center of debates about the quality of education, it would seem that UNESCO could and should be able to offer considerably more. Evidence has accumulated from a variety of sources that economic growth, even in the poorest countries, is highly dependent on the learning and cognitive skills that children acquire in primary school and that parents' literacy is one of the most important guarantors of children's success in school (Hanushek & Woessmann, 2009). This puts UNESCO squarely inside the policy debate of the future of education.

What are others doing in literacy? In work on reading in primary schooling, there is an increased effort to take a much closer look at the instructional process itself, especially with young children. Through new methods like the Early Grade Reading Assessment (EGRA), there has been a growth of interest in how best to consider, and act upon, learning outcomes of children in primary school, in (nearly) real-time (Gove & Wetterberg, 2011). Similarly, there are methods for adult assessment that build off of EGRA-like assessment instruments, and that can help programs to be more accountable for the learning dimension of adult education programs, with less focus on international comparability and more focus on improving literacy in specific cultural contexts (Wagner, 2010). Further, much is going on in the use of technology for adult education in developing countries that could be brought to bear on literacy improvement (Wagner & Kozma, 2005).

On the policy side, there may be new partnerships that UNESCO could explore in literacy work, in closer association with institutions of higher education and international agencies, in order to be a more credible thought leader. UNESCO could reconsider its global mission by building better bridges between agencies of both developed and developing countries (Heyneman, 2011). For example, all countries are interested in improving learning outcomes, providing better real-time information for policy-making, and deploying the effective use of new technologies. Finding common purposes among diverse countries—both rich and poor—would be an additional way to mobilize not only the needed fiscal resources, but intellectual ones as well. Literacy programs receive only 1% of the education budget in many countries (UNESCO, 2005). A combined program between OECD and UNESCO, for example, would be a natural option when thinking about programs that combine the interests of wealthy and poor countries. Of course, making partnerships work synergistically is always easier said than done. And, in the past, some agencies have made it difficult (or at least more complicated) for UNESCO to carry out its mission in literacy.

In the end analysis, UNESCO and the adult literacy and adult learning fields need each other. Serious concerns exist about UNESCO's literacy work, such as in the case of international literacy statistics, or delays in carrying out planned programs of work. These are not simply complaints about resources or institutional reorganization (two rationales invoked to explain such problems), even though they, too, seem to exist. Rather, there are issues of professionalism and scientific rigor that need greater attention in UNESCO's programming. UNESCO can and must help focus professional attention on literacy that the field desperately needs. Two decades ago, it was said that UNESCO "pursues its intellectual, normative, and operational commitments in a way that virtually guarantees limited impact on all fronts" (Jones, 1990, p. 58). Unfortunately, this comment is still made today.

The United Nations Literacy Decade will finish in 2013, 15 years after the *Hamburg Declaration*. Before reaching that point, there is time for a rededication of effort and focus. UNESCO will need to reassert itself not only as the agency that keeps the literacy and adult learning flame lit, but also as the agency to which the world turns for technical leadership, innovation, and access to expertise within and across nations.

References

Ercikan, K., Arim, R., Oliveri, M., & Sandilands, D. (2008). *Evaluation of the Literacy Assessment and Monitoring Programme (LAMP)/UNESCO Institute for Statistics*. Document IOS/EVS/PI/91. Montreal, Canada: UIS.

Gove, A., & Wetterberg, A. (2011). *The Early Grade Reading Assessment: Applications and interventions to improve basic literacy*. Research Triangle Park, NC: RTI.

Hanushek, E., & Woessmann, L. (2009). *Do better schools lead to more growth? Cognitive skills, economic outcomes, and causation* (Working Paper 14633). Washington, DC: National Bureau of Economic Research.

Heyneman, S. P. (2011). The future of UNESCO: Strategies for attracting new resources. *International Journal of Educational Development, 31*, 313–314.

Jones, P. W. (1990). UNESCO and the politics of global literacy. *Comparative Education Review, 34*(1), 41–60.

Jones, P. W. (1997). The World Bank and the literacy question: Orthodoxy, heresy and ideology. *International Review of Education, 34*(1), 41–60.

Limage, L. (2007). Organizational challenges to international cooperation for literacy in UNESCO. *Comparative Education, 43*(3), 451–468.

Limage, L. (2009). Multilateral cooperation for literacy promotion under stress: Governance and management issues. *Literacy and Numeracy, 17*(2), 5–33.

OECD. (2000). *Literacy in the information age: Final report of the International Adult Literacy Survey*. Paris, France: Author.

Robinson, C. (2005). *Languages and literacies*. Paris, France: UNESCO.

Smyth, J. A. (2005). *UNESCO's international literacy statistics 1950–2000.* Paris, France: UNESCO.

UNESCO. (1975, September). *Declaration of Persepolis.* Presented at the International Symposium for Literacy, Persepolis.

UNESCO. (1978). *Towards a methodology for projecting rates of literacy and educational attainment.* Paris, France: Author.

UNESCO. (1990). *World declaration on education for all.* Paris, France: Author.

UNESCO. (1997). *The Hamburg Declaration on adult learning and agenda for the future.* Paris, France: Author.

UNESCO. (2005). *Literacy for life.* EFA Global Monitoring Report. Paris, France: Author.

UNESCO. (2010). *Reaching the marginalized.* EFA Global Monitoring Report. Paris, France: Author.

UNESCO Institute for Lifelong Learning. (2009). *Harnessing the power and potential of adult learning and education for a viable future: Belém framework for action.* Hamburg, Germany: Author.

UNESCO Institute for Statistics. (2009). *The next generation of literacy statistics: Implementing the Literacy Assessment and Monitoring Programme (LAMP).* Montreal, Canada: Author.

UNESCO/UNDP (1976). *The experimental world literacy programme: A critical assessment.* Paris, France: UNESCO.

United Nations (2002). *Resolution 56/116 on United Nations Literacy Decade.* New York, NY: Author.

Wagner, D. A. (1990). Literacy assessment in the Third World: An overview and proposed schema for survey use. *Comparative Education Review, 33*(1), 112–138.

Wagner, D. A. (1992). *Literacy: Developing the future.* UNESCO Yearbook of Education. Paris, France: UNESCO.

Wagner, D. A. (2000). *Literacy and adult education.* Global Thematic Review prepared for the U.N. World Education Forum, Dakar, Senegal.

Wagner, D. A. (2010). Quality of education, comparability, and assessment choice in developing countries. *Compare: A Journal of Comparative and International Education, 40*(6), 741–760.

Wagner, D. A. (2011). What happened to literacy? Historical and conceptual perspectives on literacy in UNESCO. *International Journal of Educational Development, 31,* 319–323.

Wagner, D. A., & Kozma, R. (2005). *New technologies for literacy and adult education: A global perspective.* Paris, France: UNESCO.

Wagner, D. A., & Srivastava, A. B. L. (1989). *Measuring literacy through household surveys.* (Doc. No. DP/UN/INT-88-X01/10E). New York, NY: United Nations Statistical Office.

DANIEL WAGNER *is the UNESCO chair in learning and literacy and professor of education at the University of Pennsylvania. He is director of the International Literacy Institute and of the University of Pennsylvania's International Educational Development Program (IEDP) in graduate study.*

This chapter considers Theme 4 of the Hamburg Declaration: *Adult learning, gender equality and equity, and the empowerment of women.*

3

Adult Education of Women for Social Transformation: Reviving the Promise, Continuing the Struggle

Nelly P. Stromquist

This chapter has a fourfold purpose. It begins with a review of the balance of progress to date in conceptualizing gender. Second, it examines the objectives of CONFINTEA V and VI from a gender perspective. Third, it assesses the impact of CONFINTEA V and the *Hamburg Declaration*. Fourth, it analyzes the likely path of future state action on adult education.

Gender is a system of tangible as well as subtle oppression that, building on social constructions of femininity and masculinity, permeates institutional practices and individual beliefs in ways that render the asymmetrical distribution of freedom and power a "natural" and uncontested reality. Gender inequalities have now been reframed as an issue of human rights. But as Eisler (1987) remarks, theories of human rights and women's rights have historically developed in two separate theoretical strains, with men defined as autonomous individuals and women as caregivers. This conceptualization is erroneous, and gender justice must therefore undergo a rethinking and reconstructing of the public/private relationship (Blackmore & Kenway, 1993). Although gender touches multiple axes of subordination, it is also a force in itself, one that cuts across all other social markers.

Gender justice is a newly emerging concept. Richer than the notion of gender equality, it considers fairness as more than simply numerical parity. Fraser (2007) proposes a useful dual strategy to work on gender issues: *recognition* of the importance and legitimacy of gender differences, so that femininity is not devalued and women are not relegated to subordinate positions, and *redistribution*, by which equitable access to material goods and changes in the sexual division of labor would be part of gender transformation. She makes it

New Directions for Adult and Continuing Education, no. 138, Summer 2013 © 2013 Wiley Periodicals, Inc.
Published online in Wiley Online Library (wileyonlinelibrary.com) • DOI: 10.1002/ace.20051

clear that "claims for recognition cannot be insulated from each other" (p. 32). She further asserts that cultural norms that deny women recognition and redistribution are not acceptable. Recognition in the form of numerical representation (parity in certain spheres of social life, particularly education) is much easier to attain than redistribution. The former has the advantage of fitting democratic norms regarding participation while simultaneously not threatening the material wealth or comfort of dominant classes. Recognition is problematic for ruling elites, inasmuch as it means acknowledging that differences can be valuable. This, in turn, challenges existing hierarchies that make the world so predictable but also so oppressive to those in subordinate positions. Redistribution is even more problematic, because resources given to a disadvantaged group must often be taken away from those who are better off.

Specifically, redistribution calls for more equitable reallocations of, for example, occupations, salaries, and prestige. This would enhance competition (many new areas would become equally open to women and men) and potentially lead to the loss of some positions that men currently fill (undeniably, redistribution is a zero-sum game). Reallocation of wealth, in a proactive sense, means giving women access to land, credit, technology, better salaries, and greater freedom in the private sphere. Critically, although not apparently salient, it also implies a redistribution of the domestic division of labor. Although these changes may not produce additional revenues, they do call for the reallocation of time and effort that some men might find difficult in their personal lives.

Educational attributes can bring women both recognition and (in the longer term) redistribution. But this change is not automatic. Gender is a fundamental social marker deeply engrained in most societies. Moreover, it is a structure that creates persistent inequalities and disadvantages, mostly borne by women. Education for gender transformation needs much greater awareness of the *relevant* content and process of knowledge development and acquisition that can be fostered. Solid treatment of gender issues would incorporate content about how the social relations of gender are activated and experienced in society by both women and men; it would also include content about what collective and institutional strategies can be put in place to alter such conditions. Despite the complexity of gender transformation, there is a marked tendency today to trivialize the plight of women by merely adding gender to a list of other social disadvantages. Note this statement in the *Belém Framework for Action,* arising from CONFINTEA VI: "There can be no exclusion arising from age, gender, ethnicity, migrant status, language, religion, disability, rurality, sexual identity or orientation, poverty, displacement or imprisonment" (UNESCO Institute for Lifelong Learning, 2009, p. 40). Although the list of these disadvantages is long—it recognizes a multitude of groups that suffer discrimination in society—the simplistic addition of gender to other social markers undermines the pervasive and often severe nature of social and economic oppression linked to gender that, again, affects roughly half of those in each of the other categories.

CONFINTEA's Multiple Promises

CONFINTEA V represented a major milestone with its detailed attention to gender issues, especially in fostering empowerment through knowledge. CONFINTEA VI further developed the gender-related objectives to be accomplished through nonformal education (NFE). In additional UNESCO conferences on human rights, population and development, and the environment, women have played an enormous role in facilitating an understanding of gender issues and developing social networks to disseminate information and provide support. However, the two previous CONFINTEA conferences stand in direct contrast to each other.

Theme 4 of the *Hamburg Declaration* specifically addressed gender issues. The fruit of prolonged deliberation, the theme is worth quoting in full:

We commit ourselves to promoting the empowerment of women and gender equity through adult learning:

(a) by recognizing and correcting the continued marginalization and denial of access and of equal opportunities for quality education that girls and women are still facing at all levels;

(b) by ensuring that all women and men are provided with the necessary education to meet their basic needs and to exercise their human rights;

(c) by raising the consciousness of girls and boys, women and men concerning gender inequalities and the need to change these unequal relations;

(d) by eliminating gender disparities in access to all areas and levels of education;

(e) by ensuring that policies and practices comply with the principle of equitable representation of both sexes, especially at the managerial and decision-making level of educational programmes;

(f) by combating domestic and sexual violence through providing appropriate education for men and supplying information and counselling to increase women's ability to protect themselves from such violence;

(g) by removing barriers to access to formal and non-formal education in the case of pregnant adolescents and young mothers;

(h) by promoting a gender-sensitive participatory pedagogy which acknowledges the daily life experience of women and recognizes both cognitive and affective outcomes;

(i) by educating men and women to acknowledge the serious and adverse impacts of globalization and structural adjustment policies in all parts of the world, especially upon women;

New Directions for Adult and Continuing Education • DOI: 10.1002/ace

(j) by taking adequate legislative, financial and economic measures and by implementing social policies to ensure women's successful participation in adult education through the removal of obstacles and the provision of supportive learning environments;

(k) by educating women and men in such a way as to promote the sharing of multiple workloads and responsibilities;

(l) by encouraging women to organize as women to promote a collective identity and to create women's organizations to bring about change;

(m) by promoting women's participation in decision-making processes and in formal structures. (UNESCO, 1997, pp. 18–19)

These strategies situate women's education in a decidedly political context. Not only is the term empowerment clearly linked to the advancement of women, but also the conditions of women are embedded in the wider and stronger principle of human rights. The strategies call for a transformative education that treats participants in adult education as agents who need to develop a broad political understanding of how macro-level forces such as globalization and structural adjustment affect their lives. Further, the strategies identify two persistent issues that figure among the strongest negative practices facing women: domestic and sexual violence.

In contrast, CONFINTEA VI's final document, the *Belèm Framework for Action* (UNESCO Institute for Lifelong Learning, 2009), no longer discusses adult education through "themes" but rather offers "recommendations" along seven lines: adult literacy; policy; governance; financing; participation, inclusion and equity; quality; and monitoring its own implementation. Remarkably, empowerment does not appear as a key issue. Not only is the concept of empowerment no longer connected specifically to gender action, it also appears only once in the document. Further, it is applied to *all* adult learners, thereby losing the intent to create agency among women as a subordinate group. The closest the document comes to a treatment of gender occurs under the rubric of "participation, inclusion and equity," where the document makes reference to the need to consider the "gender-specific life-course in a full range of adult learning and education programmes for women" (p. 40). In this context—in which neither empowerment nor consciousness-raising is mentioned—the "gender-specific life-course" education seems to imply more the reproductive roles of women.

Also, the *Belèm Framework for Action* no longer identifies any specific problems women face. Moreover, it endorses the literacy goals stated in *Education for All* (EFA) and in the *Millennium Development Goals* (MDG) (United Nations, 2010) but fails to question their downgrading of literacy. For example, this latter document no longer claims that the reduction of adult illiteracy is a major objective, nor even a target, but rather an *indicator* linked to both the achievement of universal primary education and the promotion of gender equality and women's empowerment. Moreover, already weakened as a call to action, adult literacy is further narrowed in the MDG to people aged between 15 and 24, thus ignoring a large population of illiterate parents of school-age children (that is, those in the 25–40-year-old group) who in their efforts to become literate through adult education could play a decisive role in breaking the intergenerational transmission of low education. A focus on the 15–24 age group totally disregards the needs that women over the age of 25 have in their daily lives, in their own education, and in the reform of conventional gender roles into which both women and men are socialized.

Further, the priorities expressed in the *Belèm Framework for Action* include the need for more data on adult education programs, for increased monitoring of their implementation, for greater professional training of adult educators, and for more funding. These are, however, overall objectives and move toward a concern for quality—which is highly welcome—but away from the specificity of gender issues. The document takes a decisive step in its emphasis on "lifelong learning" but does not discuss what differences in meaning lifelong learning would have for women and men, especially those who find themselves destitute. In sum, CONFINTEA VI does not advance the education of women. On the contrary, it takes the political edge off CONFINTEA V by instead proposing vague recommendations.

The Empirical Evidence on Government Action

Three pieces of evidence can be used to assess the impact of the *Hamburg Declaration*: a midterm report based on 16 countries conducted by an educational NGO (International Council for Adult Education [ICAE], 2003), a midterm report produced on the basis of governmental documentation (UNESCO, 2003), and the 154 country reports presented to UNESCO in preparation for CONFINTEA VI.

The ICAE report found that several new programs have been developed under the influence of CONFINTEA V, but none involved gender. It also found that data separated by gender were missing in a number of countries, as was data that cross-referenced gender by rural/urban residence or ethnicity. During the five years of national action in response to CONFINTEA V, the literacy gap between women and men was reduced in only one of the 16 selected countries. Few nations reported post-literacy programs. Among the developing countries in the study, government investment in adult education varied considerably but was very small, ranging from US$3 per capita in Zambia to US$0.40 per capita in Jamaica. The study also found that despite frequent discourse on human rights and empowerment, coverage of such issues is "still not part of formal or nonformal programmes in some of the countries selected" (ICAE, 2003, p. 74). Noting that "since it was so difficult to gather concrete data" on interventions and concrete programs, it concluded that "serious doubts have to be cast on the real implementation of this discourse" (p. 125).

New Directions for Adult and Continuing Education • DOI: 10.1002/ace

The UNESCO midterm report was produced on the basis of thematic workshops, one of which dealt with gender. Although it was very brief and did not deal with specific countries or programs, it estimated that the EFA literacy goal would not be reached by 2015. Nevertheless, it still managed to assert that there had been "significant advances in the empowerment of women" (UNESCO, 2003, p. 18). In recent years, UNESCO has increased its capacity to gather reports from its member countries on their progress in developing adult education. Consequently, in preparation for CONFINTEA VI most countries were asked to submit national reports on recent national developments. Curious about what had been accomplished since 1997, I reviewed 12 national reports (three each from the Arab States, Africa, Asia, and Latin America and the Caribbean). Overwhelmingly, these reports tend to reduce adult education to mere literacy. Only three of the national reports indicate that they have post-literacy programs for adults, and only two refer to the need for women's empowerment. When courses available to women are listed, they cover issues like hygiene, health education, and the environment, suggesting a practical focus rather than a transformative content. However, more positively, a number of countries report having specific units that deal with gender issues within their governmental structure.

As is the case for the informal sector of the economy—seldom recognized for its overwhelming impact in the developing world—adult education continues to be invisible in national development efforts. The 12 national reports do not consistently state the proportion of the educational budget that goes to adult education; those that do indicate a range from 0.5 to 3.7%. Also, the content of these reports varies considerably, and none of them follows a format that enables their reader to trace the 13 actions of the *Hamburg Declaration*'s theme on promoting women's empowerment. Often, the national reports do not present basic adult education enrollment statistics disaggregated by gender between 1997 (the year of CONFINTEA V) and 2008 (the year in which the final reports were presented), which makes it difficult to assess progress over time. Some of the documents indicate NGO involvement in the provision of adult education programs; none identifies to what extent the participation of women-led NGOs has been taking place.

Thus, we can conclude from reading the selected national reports that there is limited attention to adult education and even less gender awareness in the adult education programs of many countries. Their discourse (and that expressed in the various other official documents of international conferences) underwent minimal translation into operational levels.

A Predictable Path and Possibilities for Escaping It

Why does such dissonance between policy and action continue? National governments gain legitimacy in the eyes of their citizens and in the international arena when they show interest in the conditions of their people. International

New Directions for Adult and Continuing Education • DOI: 10.1002/ace

conferences like CONFINTEA create major venues for both the production of gender knowledge and its dissemination. These occur through the oral exchanges and efforts during the drafting and presentation of conference documents, during which points of agreement or disagreement among participating country representatives and civil society members are expressed. Even though these documents are rarely translated into action in the countries endorsing them, the official discourse itself represents a formal—though nonbinding—agreement that can be used to a government's benefit in the public sphere. Of course, it is easy to then assign lower levels of priority to adult education as poor populations can exert only weak leverage.

In preparation for the Rio+20 United Nations Conference on Sustainable Development, a virtual exchange of views took place in June 2012 that centered on the accomplishments of CONFINTEA V and the policy shifts that CONFINTEA VI could bring (Education Working Group, 2012). Many educators taking part asserted that adult education today needs less planning and more concrete action to realize the multiple aims of the *Hamburg Declaration*. It is tragic that many of the goals endorsed by the global community of countries, international agencies, and NGOs in 1997 repeat themselves time after time with only modest attainment of such goals. *The Future We Want* (UN, 2012), the final document of the Rio+20 conference representing the consensus of all participating governments, ended up with a language that, being acceptable to all signatories, eliminated any controversial demands. It clearly recognizes the importance of human rights and makes repeated reference to *gender equality* and *women's empowerment*. It has one section on education and another on gender and women's empowerment. However, the discussion of NFE appears linked only to "youth" promotion, not to women (p. 41), and the section on gender makes no mention of the potential role of women-led NGOs and leaves the question of funding primarily in the hands of international organizations, regional banks, and the private sector (p. 42). The Rio document can be taken as yet another instance where rhetorical recognition of gender justice and equality is strong, but the document is weak in crafting the strategies to make that commitment a reality.

A transformative gender role can be expected from women-led NGOs, since women are the most likely advocates for their own advancement. Women-led NGOs participate constantly in efforts to change their respective societies and also play crucial roles in monitoring policy implementation so that official discourses are aligned with any subsequent implementation. Women in these institutions and networks not only express demands for change but also create knowledge through the processes of framing problems and formulating solutions. In other words, significant informal learning occurs. Regrettably, this particular contribution to knowledge development often tends to be unrecognized by educational and social science policy makers and researchers.

Feminist monitoring of actions taken by important international agencies and think tanks also serves a key function in the production of knowledge and its dissemination. One recent example of this, reflecting more defensive than proactive action by women-led NGOs, concerns the Global Compact on Learning led by the UNESCO Institute of Statistics and the Brookings Institute. They have established a learning metrics task force to identify learning goals and targets regarding early, primary, and post-primary learning. Feminist activists have expressed concern with its emphasis on measuring learning while neglecting the impacts of learning on outcomes such as empowered citizenship, political participation, community leadership, decent work, and sustainable livelihoods (Castillo, 2012). One additional concern is that the Global Compact on Learning centers entirely on formal schooling, thus again contributing to the marginalization of NFE and adult women.

Work on the adult education of women continues primarily through the efforts of women-led organizations—efforts characterized by insufficient funding and much sweat and tears for small achievements. An important question concerns who are the women who can work on their behalf? Some insights can be drawn from the massive surveys (with a sample size of over 33,000 respondents) conducted in Latin America in recent years (see Lynch, Render, & Twoney, 2012). The empirical evidence continues to confirm existing knowledge that political participation solidifies democratic practices by transmitting civic skills and showing participants that action leads to government responsiveness. The study by Lynch and associates (2012) explored whether political participation is a matter of wealth (that is, having more time, resources, and networks to engage in political activities) or a matter of need (that is, facing considerable problems in one's community). It found that need has a greater association with participation than wealth and that participation was positively associated with education. These results confirmed previous findings that citizens with greater knowledge of both the political system and greater skills to engage in political action tend to participate more than do their counterparts with less education. While acknowledging that people are motivated to engage in political action to solve some of their needs, another study brings more caution to this finding. Pereira (2012), using data from the same massive Latin American survey, found a strong correlation between low local participation in the solution of neighborhood/community problems and being a homemaker with children at home. Time devoted to the private sphere limits the available time for the public sphere, even in contexts of great need. In other words, the social actors most likely to favor changing gender relations are the same ones who face the most constraints when engaging in political action.

Conclusions

If transformative education is to be fostered, the role of adult education is essential. Equally essential is the participation of women, who must constitute themselves as agents of their own advancement and help break the intergenerational transmission of detrimental traditional values. However, although

New Directions for Adult and Continuing Education • DOI: 10.1002/ace

the discussion and acceptance of gender issues in adult education programs is now more common, three major obstacles still exist. First, globalization's ethos of national competitiveness assigns an overwhelming importance to formal approaches to education—in particular their scientific and technological aspects—to the detriment of nonformal education and informal learning. Second, adult education remains a stagnant, sleepy area of policy that continues to be underfunded. It is also an area in which too little research is conducted, which further weakens its visibility. Third, the role of the strongest advocates for the transformation of gender relations is not yet fully recognized or incorporated into community and national efforts.

These obstacles are not insurmountable. What is needed is the collective resolve of those who have benefited from formal education to recognize the plight and urgency of adult education for those who have been and continue to be marginalized. Governments must be made accountable by international organizations and bilateral agencies rather than treated with kid gloves. Finally, a return to the goals and specific actions identified in the *Hamburg Declaration* is sorely needed. All are minimum demands for those who subscribe to democracy and social justice.

References

Blackmore, J., & Kenway, J. (Eds.). (1993). *Gender matters in educational administration and policy: A feminist introduction.* London, England: Falmer Press.

Castillo, R. (2012, June). *The cloth of life?* Virtual exchange organized by ICA. Global discussion on achievements, challenges, and the future of EFA to reach EFA targets of 2015 and shape post-2015 international education agenda.

Education Working Group. (2012). *The education for the world we want. Campana por el Derecho a la Educacion.* Retrieved from http://www.Campanaderechoeducacion.org /participacion/?=568

Eisler, R. (1987). Human rights: Toward an integrated theory for action. *Gender Issues, 17*(1), 25–46.

Fraser, N. (2007). Feminist politics in the age of recognition: A two-dimensional approach to social justice. *Studies in Social Justice, 1*(1), 23–35.

International Council for Adult Education. (2003). *Agenda for the future: Six years later.* Montevideo, Uruguay: Author.

Lynch, M., Render, S., & Twoney, M. (2012). Asking for help in the Americas: The importance of needs, efficacy, and political engagement. *Americas Barometers Insights, 81*, 1–10.

Pereira, F. (2012). Gender and community participation in Latin America and the Caribbean. *Americas Barometers Insights, 78*, 1–9.

UNESCO. (1997). *The Hamburg Declaration on adult learning and agenda for the future.* Paris, France: Author.

UNESCO. (2003). *Synthesis report on the CONFINTEA V midterm review meeting.* Hamburg, Germany: Author.

UNESCO Institute for Lifelong Learning. (2009). *Harnessing the power and potential of adult learning and education for a viable future: Belém framework for action.* Hamburg, Germany: Author.

United Nations. (2010). *Millennium development goals.* New York, NY: Author.

United Nations. (2012). *The future we want.* New York, NY: Author.

NELLY P. STROMQUIST *is a professor in the international education policy program, College of Education, at the University of Maryland. Her research addresses gender issues, educational change, and the impact of globalization on higher education.*

4

This chapter examines Theme 5 of the Hamburg Declaration: *Adult learning and the changing world of work.*

From the Quixotic to the Pragmatic: The *Hamburg Declaration*, Adult Education, and Work

Amy Rose

The *Hamburg Declaration* (UNESCO, 1997) is perhaps most quixotic and prescient in laying out the changing world of work as envisioned in 1997. It includes particular commitments to promote the rights to work and to work-related adult learning, to increase access to work-related adult learning for different target groups, and to diversify "the contents of work-related adult learning" (p. 20). Over the past 12 years, we have seen instead the development of a completely bifurcated system: a conceptual shift from work as a place to work as the result of effort. For those with technical skills, the shifts in the notion of work and learning have been pronounced. However, those without technical skills are now even further away from the kind of integration envisioned.

The document was prescient in its concern for the loss of workers' rights, but it could not have foreseen the recession of 2008 and after. It envisioned a static world in which learning could be incorporated into all aspects of the contemporary workplace. In particular this included implementing literacy programs, increasing access for women and minorities, ensuring workplace safety, and "enriching the learning environment" in the workplace.

So what has happened since 1997? Have any of these commitments been met? How has the world of work changed? Has it become more hospitable to learning? It is clear that the broad goals of the *Hamburg Declaration* are not a priority for much of the corporate world. Industry has retreated from many of its "non-essential" activities, nor does it make training a high priority. Further, many of the work-related concerns of the *Hamburg Declaration* were completely absent from the CONFINTEA VI agenda (UNESCO Institute for

New Directions for Adult and Continuing Education, no. 138, Summer 2013 © 2013 Wiley Periodicals, Inc.
Published online in Wiley Online Library (wileyonlinelibrary.com) • DOI: 10.1002/ace.20052

Lifelong Learning, 2009). In part the change came from the decision to focus on policy and basic education. However, it seems that the trends of the past decade indicate a shift to emphasizing workforce preparation while only paying lip service to lifelong learning and continuing education. This chapter will examine some of the trends indicated in the *Declaration* and show some examples of the ways workplace learning has incorporated these trends into learning situations. It is particularly telling that innovation as the source of industrial growth was not included within the parameters of the *Declaration*, at least in terms of workplace commitments.

Globalization and Changing Work Relationships

Globalization and changing work relationships have been key issues in discussions of economic change for about 20 years. Globalization is a ubiquitous term, but in essence it can "be conceptualized as the movement of goods, services, and information across national boundaries and as a borderless marketplace shored up by what is being called the knowledge economy" (Merriam, 2010, p. 402). One key part of globalization is a shift among developed countries to a knowledge economy. Such countries no longer trade goods, but rather information and services. Writers extolling the strengths of globalization point precisely to the de-emphasis of national boundaries, the movement of the educated across national boundaries and a concomitant increase in diversity within workforces around the world.

However, globalization is also now regarded as a problem as well as a positive phenomenon. It was initially envisioned as containing the possibility for improving work life and creating social equality. However, there is a central paradox here. The writers of the *Hamburg Declaration* saw the potential dangers of globalization, predicting a world of continuing regionalization and specialization, while nevertheless embracing the possibilities of regional cooperation and economic growth. Even so, they never envisioned the shift away from structured workplace learning toward either the outsourcing of both work and learning or the increasing emphasis on self-direction. In this case, despite lip service to lifelong learning, the mandate of the *Hamburg Declaration* has basically been relegated to the truism that only those who have education are entitled to more. The integration of work and learning as incorporated in the *Declaration* was truly visionary, but the reality of the world 15 years later is that the goals of collaboration, integration of learning, and the democratic workplace have been lost.

A concomitant development has been the growth of the contingent workforce and the loosening of what have been called traditional workplace commitments. In other words, new globalized corporations have a different perception of the workforce as an asset. It is now seen as a resource or an aspect of interchangeable capital. Although this concept is derived from Schultz's (1960) idea of human capital, it is even more extreme. Lewchuk, Clarke, and de Wolf (2011) explore the ramifications of what they call the "erosion of permanent employment relationships" (p. 10): the trend to hire individuals as independent contractors rather than as permanent employees. Their case study examines the health of those affected by such trends. The loss of permanent employment relationships and the rise of contract work seriously affect the health of workers, their families, and communities, as well as the kinds of educational opportunities on offer to workers. Even though this trend could be seen in the late 1990s, its effects were not so widespread at that time. Indeed, Lewchuk et al. speculate that the severity of the financial crisis of 2008 was partly a result of the loosening of the commitment to workers and work relationships. Not only do contingent workers lose job security and health benefits, they also lose all possibilities for job training, growth, and even any sense of job future. Thus the vision of the *Hamburg Declaration* in this regard has been completely subverted. Not only are learning organizations no longer the wave of the future, but even minimal responsibility for training is passed on to workers or the community at large. Few possibilities for mobility exist without external educational input. This is an international trend, although the shift seems most pronounced in first-world nations.

Learning Regions

Learning regions have been an important focus of adult education since the 1970s. The concept can be considered as both an approach and a philosophical position that perhaps best embodies the ideals of the *Hamburg Declaration*. In this section I will examine what has happened to some of the better known examples, particularly that of Mondragon in Spain. Other examples include some of the integrated approaches adopted by some European and Australian municipalities. For Longworth (2006), learning regions represent an important, albeit complex, aspect of regional development. However, these efforts do not always incorporate basic education—a primary focus of the *Hamburg Declaration*—and they also deal with municipal issues rather than the broader collaborations it originally envisioned.

Discussions of learning regions are confusing because of varying definitions and approaches. Asheim (2011) lays out three ways that learning regions are conceptualized. Geographers discuss learning regions in terms of regional "cooperation and collective learning in regional clusters and networks in order to promote the innovativeness and competitiveness of firms and regions" (Asheim, 2011, p. 994). However, economists think about learning regions as the source of a commodity (knowledge) that leads to learning and the making of more knowledge. A third approach sees the learning region as "regionally based development coalitions," where development involves all sectors of society as a "bottom-up horizontally based co-operation between different actors in a local or regional setting" (Asheim, 2011, p. 994). Within this third view, the learning region is a group or collaboration among cooperating organizations and is often considered to be an important source of innovation. This idea has been adopted by educators who see learning regions as a form of workplace democratization. This idea goes beyond the clustering of resources in the geographic sense. The principal concept is that learning regions help with development, spreading wealth through knowledge gained from the geographic area and leading to collaboration. Although this idea of clustering may be effective in fostering economic growth, it is not always a catalyst in fostering equity and democratic processes.

Educators often build on this notion of networks to construct a slightly different view of learning regions and to include other localities. For example, Jarvis (2007) cites one definition of the learning city as:

> One which strives to learn how to renew itself in a period of extraordinary social change. The rapid spread of new technologies presents considerable opportunities for countries and regions to benefit from the transfer of new knowledge and ideas across national boundaries. At the same time global shifts in capital flows and production are creating uncertainties and risk in managing national and local economies. (p. 116)

Educators have drawn on this notion of the learning region or city as a nexus of networks, but they also focus on the networks' connection to continuous regional learning. This is a slightly different meaning than the geographers use, although they all draw on all of these paradigms in thinking about learning regions. Ultimately, the notion of learning is more completely tied into the view of the learning region as envisioned by educators. For example, Ron Faris defined a learning community as "a form of learning-based community development in which the concept of lifelong learning is explicitly used to mobilize the learning resources of all community sectors" (as cited in Dymock, 2007, p. 90). There is an ideal of change that suffuses this definition, yet it is not explicit. The problem is that moving beyond this vision to actual implementation has proven to be elusive. As seen through the plethora of definitions, individuals take this notion in many different directions. Ways of bringing about a learning region are, on the whole, difficult to figure out, and also ultimately questionable. We must continuously ask, "Who benefits from this?"

Thus, this third approach to the learning region is allied closely to the *Hamburg Declaration*. Learning is embedded in all aspects of production as an outcome, an asset, and a commodity. However, more recently the geographic concept of the learning region has become ascendant, while the idea of the learning region as a democratizing entity is largely ignored. Very often, this ideal of the learning region is coupled with a notion of cooperative ownership. For example, Mondragon in Spain is well known as a group of cooperatives that has functioned on a corporate level for fifty years. They have inspired much research analyzing whether democratizing principles can overcome corporate selfishness. However, the jury is still out. By 1999, Cheney was examining how their democratic work values had given way to consumerism and more efficient human resource management approaches.

New Directions for Adult and Continuing Education • DOI: 10.1002/ace

In summary, learning regions and cities have been put forward as an enticing approach in democratization and as a means of development of resources that has little to do with this and more to do with a particular approach to economic development.

Collaboration, Creativity, and Productivity

Collaboration is emphasized in the *Hamburg Declaration*. This can be seen in its calls for the multifaceted development of workers as part of the document's fundamental humanism. However, over time this humanism has become distorted: the terminology is the same, but its meaning is different. The quixotic notion of collaboration for individual development has given way to collaboration for increased profit. Some of these changes can be seen in the use of continuing education as a bargaining tool. In the United States, the Institute for Career Development (ICD) was formed in the 1990s as a partnership between the steel workers' union and the steel companies. But the partnership was focused on providing training and educational experiences for those who were leaving the industry, either through layoffs or early retirement. Recently, the ICD's funding has been cut drastically, even though the need remains as strong as ever. In the United Kingdom, a similar program focuses on a broader effort to provide educational opportunities to union members through a system of Union Learning Representatives (Union Learn, n.d.).

Collaboration can also be seen in current experiments in employee ownership. Berry and Schneider (2011) outline the ways that a workers' cooperative can work with a union to create better work conditions and better service. However, collaboration has an important subtext. It is related to ideas about creativity and innovation: the buzz words of the moment. To be sure, innovation has been a consistent issue, especially since the mid-19th century. However, in Western Europe and North America, this call for creativity is part of an effort to regain a competitive edge since manufacturing has moved to Asia, South America, and (more recently) Africa. There are some indications that increasing vertical integration of the marketplace may help move some aspects of the manufacturing process back, but others seem to be gone for good. This trend can be seen in the plethora of business books focused on creativity as a management or a vision issue. Lehrer (2012) discusses the deficiencies of scientists whose lab work failed to develop a new cleaning product. Instead, an outside group, observing the actual performance of housework, imagined a completely new approach that essentially did away with mops and cleaning materials altogether. On the other hand, Gertner (2012) lays out his view of the sources of innovation through a case study of the rise and fall of Bell Labs. In tracing its history, Gertner concludes that corporatization, increasing emphasis on short-term profits, and the loss of potential for individual idiosyncrasy led to the demise of Bell Labs. Its successor, Alcatel-Lucent, instead focused on developing an entrepreneurial spirit rather than "science and scholarship" (p. 337).

This ideal of collaboration is closely connected to both learning regions and globalization. Despite the tenets laid out in the *Hamburg Declaration*, the concept that education and work are interrelated aspects of the same phenomenon has been lost. For the uneducated, collaboration was more fully enunciated in the workers co-ops discussed earlier. There is bifurcation of effort where education and work are concerned. For the educated, the focus is on creativity and profit, but for the uneducated it is on employment and profit. However, the integration of work and learning as envisioned in the *Hamburg Declaration* is sadly missing. Instead, the focus on technology and technicality has replaced broader human concerns.

Self-Direction, E-Learning, and Technology

When the *Hamburg Declaration* was written, the current love affair with technology was well under way; however, the form it would take in the early twenty-first century was still unclear. What we can see today is that workplace learning is now almost entirely focused on ideas about self-direction and the use of technology. There is little concern with individual development and an almost total reliance on the individual as a resource. Individuals who develop themselves as resources have more of a possibility of longevity, but this possibility is not assured.

Two trends are closely connected within this notion. First, the idea of self-direction has taken hold within corporate cultures. While this is not entirely new, it is an important and growing trend within the current workplace. Corporations in particular are retreating from the concept of corporate universities. For example, until the early 2000s Motorola University was a leader among corporate universities. However, it was disbanded in the early 2000s, a victim of corporate cutbacks. Instead Motorola now uses a combination of learning contracts and self-directed learning to support training. Instead of relying on trainers, learners are encouraged to decide on their own learning and then to evaluate it. This self-directed model adopted a notion that is not predicated on increasing expertise but on incorporating core values of flexibility, resilience, and curiosity. The strongest message of this shift to self-directed learning is that learning occurs outside of the work day; it is no longer privileged through a release from work (Ellinger, 2004; Guglielmino & Durr, 2012; Guglielmino & Murdick, 1997).

Second, the trend of self-direction can be seen in contemporary emphases on e-learning and technology. Too often, these are seen as panaceas, simultaneously providing access, individualization, and as-needed learning. However, the issue is more complex. As technology potentially has a broader reach than traditional educational methods, there are advantages of time and space. However, a focus on technology excludes a vast number of workers and shifts the locus of control onto learners. While this can certainly stimulate learning, it can also cut it off. Advocates of this approach have erred in thinking that because successful managers employ self-directed learning and because self-direction correlates with creativity, self-direction causes creativity (Guglielmino et al., 2009). This leads to an emphasis on creating contexts for creativity at the expense of workplace learning that would help to even the playing field.

Career Pathways

So far, I have dealt with the broader connections between learning, education, and work. However, another trend connects learning and work through career preparation. In North America, it is common to talk about career pathways. Although strictly speaking this movement deals more with career preparation than with the integration of work and learning, some aspects are still appropriate here. The principal idea behind career pathways is the linkage between training and jobs. In particular, the current emphasis on green jobs integrates technology, career paths, and economic mobility into an enticing package. Scully-Russ (2013) points out that little evidence exists to back these claims. While policy makers envision a demand-driven job training program, few jobs have yet been produced. The green jobs movement is an excellent case. Anticipating a need for a variety of highly specialized workers in various aspects of green jobs, the United States funded major initiatives aimed at training laid-off workers for employment in green industries. Unlike some previous developments mentioned earlier, green jobs and career pathways are aimed at those with lower levels of education and skills. However, jobs have yet to materialize, and even though some interesting projects have been started, it is difficult to say where this integration of work and education will go. Most important, educating individuals for specific jobs limits their possibilities for mobility. There has been a recent realization (in some sectors) that technology alone will not drive job creation. Put another way, innovation and creativity are synonymous with broad employment. Training for the future means more than training for limited potential worksites. In a time when work-related training is being cut back or eliminated, there is little possibility for mobility or even enhancement of skills.

Finally, as the very nature of the relationship between work and learning has shifted since the time of the *Hamburg Declaration*, it is too early to tell if this shift is temporary or more permanent. While policies still focus on the need for continuous learning in the workplace, more of this learning has moved out of the workplace, and the onus for it has shifted to the individual. The ambiguous message of self-development has been replaced by a more blatant concern for the bottom line. Interestingly, the ideal of continuous learning has been superseded by a focus on innovation and creativity. For those who are highly educated already, this can be a welcome shift; however, this development raises questions about how the workplace will respond to the undereducated.

There have been cycles of expansion and retrenchment in the area of workplace learning. At the time of the *Hamburg Declaration*, there was greater optimism about aligning the interests of workers and corporations. Today, the focus is on individual self-development and prerequisite training. The emphasis on innovative practices in both product development and in manufacturing calls for a continuing message of development. However, current sources of innovation focus on individuals and workplace cultures. This approach contains an inherent contradiction. Innovation and creativity are rooted in expertise, and expertise needs to be constantly replenished, yet the means to encourage this through specific programs has receded. The connection between learning and work is both assumed and eviscerated.

In conclusion, the worldview promulgated by the *Hamburg Declaration* seems, to me at least, hopelessly outdated, insofar as it relates to the world of work. Conversely, Preece (2011) views the present mood as more positive than it was in 1997: it "has harnessed a desire to proactively effect change on an international scale. There is a great collective intensity towards world causes, toward global responses to these causes and toward the role of education for development" (p. 106). While I would not disagree with her emphases, at least within work situations, the focus has shifted from a broad integration of work and learning at all levels to one that concentrates on profit and views the worker as an expendable resource. This is a source of disappointment rather than joy.

References

Asheim, B. (2011). The changing role of learning regions in the globalizing knowledge economy: A theoretical re-examination. *Regional Studies, 46*(8), 993–1004. doi:10.1080/00343404.2011.607805

Berry, D. P., & Schneider, S. (2011). Improving the quality of home health aide jobs: A collaboration between organized labor and a worker cooperative. In E. J. Carberry (Ed.), *Employee ownership and shared capitalism: New directions in research* (pp. 59–89). Champaign, IL: Labor and Employment Relations Association.

Cheney, G. (1999). *Values at work: Employee participation meets market pressure at Mondragon.* Ithaca, NY: Cornell University Press.

Dymock, D. (2007). Exploring learning in a small rural community. In M. Osborne, M. Houston, & N. Toman (Eds.), *The pedagogy of lifelong learning: Understanding effective teaching and learning in diverse contexts* (pp. 90–101). London, England: Routledge.

Ellinger, A. D. (2004). The concept of self-directed learning and its implications for human resource development. *Advances in Developing Human Resources, 6*(2), 158–177.

Gertner, J. (2012). *The idea factory: Bell Labs and the great age of American innovation.* New York, NY: Penguin Press.

Guglielmino, L., & Durr, R. (2012, February). *Are highly self-directed learning organizations and cultures more productive?* Paper presented at the 26th International Self-Directed Learning Symposium, Cocoa Beach, FL.

Guglielmino, L., Gray, E., Le Arvary, K., Asen, J., Goldstein, D., Kamin, F., . . . Snowberger, D. (2009). Self-directed learners change our world: SDL as a force for innovation, discovery, and social change. *International Journal of Self-Directed Learning, 6*(1), 11–30.

Guglielmino, P. J., & Murdick, R. G. (1997). Self-directed learning: The quiet revolution in corporate training and development. *SAM Advanced Management Journal, 62*(3), 10–18.

Jarvis, P. (2007). *Globalisation, lifelong learning and the learning society: Sociological perspectives.* New York, NY: Routledge.

Lehrer, J. (2012). *Imagine: How creativity works.* Boston, MA: Houghton Mifflin Harcourt.

Lewchuk, W., Clarke, M., & de Wolf, A. (2011). *Working without commitments: The health effects of precarious employment.* Montreal, Canada: McGill-Queen's University Press.

Longworth, N. (2006). *Learning cities, learning regions, learning communities: Lifelong learning and local government.* London, England: Routledge.

Merriam, S. B. (2010). Globalization and the role of adult and continuing education: Challenges and opportunities. In C. Kasworm, A. D. Rose, & J. Ross-Gordon (Eds.), *Handbook of adult and continuing education: 2010 edition* (pp. 401–409). Thousand Oaks, CA: Sage Publications.

Preece, J. (2011). Research in adult education and lifelong learning in the era of CONFINTEA VI. *International Journal of Lifelong Education, 30*(1), 99–117.

Schultz, T. W. (1960). Capital formation by education. *Journal of Political Economy, 68*(6), 571–583.

Scully-Russ, E. (2013). Are green jobs career pathways a path to a 21st century workforce development system? *Adult Learning, 24*(1), 6–13.

UNESCO. (1997). *The Hamburg Declaration on adult learning and agenda for the future.* Paris, France: Author.

UNESCO Institute for Lifelong Learning. (2009). *Harnessing the power and potential of adult learning and education for a viable future: Belém framework for action.* Hamburg, Germany: Author.

Union Learn. (n.d.). *Union learning reps.* Retrieved from http://www.unionlearn.org.uk /about-unionlearn/union-learning-reps

AMY ROSE is the 2012–2013 William Allen Endowed Chair and Distinguished Professor at Seattle University and professor emerita at Northern Illinois University. She writes on the history and policy of adult education.

5

This chapter considers Theme 6 of the Hamburg Declaration: *Adult learning in relation to environment, health and population.*

Adult Learning, Education, and the Environment

Darlene E. Clover, Robert Hill

The environment is now a common theme in adult education. However, conversations that swirled around the United Nations Conference on Sustainable Development (Rio+20) in June 2012 suggested major environmental challenges persist, demanding that education, learning, advocacy and activism be augmented to ensure the survival of the planet. Indeed, most social media messages from the conference lamented the continuing deep geographical (West versus the rest) and ideological divisions hampering the search for global environmental solutions. Despite efforts by organizations such as the International Council for Adult Education (ICAE), major political and policy commitments to change were weak at best. The United States played a singular role as the sniper at the Earth Summit in Rio in 1992. Egeland (as cited in Amnesty International, 2012, p. 1) reports that the "G77 countries, the Holy See, and Canada formed a shameful alliance against making a commitment to human rights, on occasion aided by the US. Despite opposition, rights language has survived in the outcome document but it does not go far enough."

Neoliberalism and capitalism powerfully interfere with those on the global stage who have little control but much-needed natural resources. Enforced consumerism is extolled as nationalism—things are to be consumed, combusted, exhausted, replaced, and discarded at a constantly accelerating pace to ensure economic prosperity above all else. A propagandist discourse of "ethical oil" fills the airwaves between devastating oil spills; environmental justice is shouted from rooftops but ignored in board rooms; and women, often the poorest of the poor who work harder to care for children poisoned by contamination, remain collateral damage in the pursuit of profit at any cost.

NEW DIRECTIONS FOR ADULT AND CONTINUING EDUCATION, no. 138, Summer 2013 © 2013 Wiley Periodicals, Inc.
Published online in Wiley Online Library (wileyonlinelibrary.com) • DOI: 10.1002/ace.20053

49

In adult education, Walter (2009) argues that despite years of environmental movements and activity at local, regional, and international levels, we
are still not particularly green in terms of "research and scholarship" (p. 4).
This chapter explores such concerns from the context of Theme 6 of the
Hamburg Declaration (UNESCO, 1997). Although it focuses particularly on
the environment, it also addresses its intersections with the related concerns
of population and health.

Within these issues, although all is not well, neither is all lost. The world
has come a great distance in terms of ecological and environmental consciousness, and there has been some change since 1972, when the United Nations
held the first conference on the environment. Examples abound: much elec-
tricity in Denmark comes from wind power, recycling programs proliferate,
and environmental activism worldwide soars to daring and creative heights.
The late Wangari Muta Maathai, a visionary African adult educator, was beaten
and jailed for her activism but still awarded the 2004 Nobel Peace Prize for
linking the environment with gender, human rights, health (HIV/AIDS), poverty, and population (Kushner, 2009). Many European countries now have
green parties as part of coalition governments that advocate education for
democratic processes, the end of corporate control of life systems, healthy
environments, economic and social justice, population awareness, and non-
violence in all its forms. And indigenous peoples in countries such as Canada
have used United Nations declarations on cultural rights to their advantage
(Clover, 2011).

The 1997 Hamburg conference marked the first time that environmental
issues were included on a CONFINTEA conference agenda. Although lacking
the same prominence, they remained on the agenda of CONFINTEA VI in
2009 (but played a much more powerful role in the International Council for
Adult Education's [ICAE] preparatory work, especially during the International
Civil Society Forum [FISC]). Adult educators were also on the frontline of
struggle at Rio+20. Seldom would anyone utter the extraordinarily naïve
statement of an adult educator at the 1992 CASAE conference: "So you are an
adult educator working on the environment? Now, that would be about trees
wouldn't it?" However, Hill and colleagues (2008) have pointed out that the
U.S. academic contribution to CONFINTEA VI devastatingly served a neoliberal agenda—the reduction of adult education and learning to basic literacy
workforce preparation shunned the "greening" of the discourse. Lastly, in its
discussions of CONFINTEA conferences as well as other UNESCO initiatives,
a recent issue of *Adult Learning* (Alfred, 2011) unproblematically reproduces
adult education's complicity with eschewing ecological issues and falls prey to
the educational industrial complex and U.S. bureaucratic interests.

With these contrasting images of our world and our field today, this
chapter reflects on where we were and where we need to go in the area of
environmental adult education. We begin with a selective discussion of the
main United Nations conferences on the environment and environmental education since 1972 to provide a historical sketch of the tumultuous global

New Directions for Adult and Continuing Education • DOI: 10.1002/ace

political canvas on which we continue to draw. From this we briefly discuss the philosophical ideas captured in the CONFINTEA V and VI documents (UNESCO, 1997; UNESCO Institute for Lifelong Learning, 2009). We then shift to a discussion of Rio+20 (United Nations, 2012) and conclude by focusing on some of the key directions in which environmental adult education and learning must head if it is to support people's actions in contesting and exercising power in the neoliberal ecological landscape. Throughout, we argue that while adult educators do not necessarily have to take the lead, it is imperative that they are part of the struggle.

From the "Human" Environment to Climate Change

Both the United Nations and UNESCO organize international conferences based on a belief that they can change thinking and approaches or set new agendas. Politically speaking, the United Nations environmental conferences have been on somewhat of a downward spiral, punctuated with positive spikes, that impacts adult education to varying degrees. In 1972 the United Nations organized in Sweden the first ever space for open debate on the environment, the *Conference on the Human Environment*. It acknowledged that the environment affects people's well-being and that its destruction is harmful to the physical, mental, and social health of humankind. Although education is mentioned in this document, adult educators were absent due to little acknowledgment of the importance of environmental issues in the field (Clover, 1999).

In *The Stockholm Declaration* (United Nations, 1972) neoliberalism only hovered in the background, not yet gripping the world in the way it does today. For an example of the change, the second United Nations Conference on Environment and Development (Earth Summit), which was held in Rio de Janeiro, Brazil, in 1992, replaced "human" with "development," emphasizing the "new world order" of consumption for prosperity epitomized in the comment by George H. W. Bush: "The American consumer lifestyle is not up for discussion. . . . Now about that 'vision' thing." Despite much lobbying, protests, and overt and covert activities by civil society organizations to challenge the development paradigm, the environment was wrenched from the discourse of human rights and placed securely within the unmitigated confines of the global trade agenda. The environment thus became a commodity, not a right for dignity and life.

However, *Agenda 21* (United Nations, 1992) was a relatively robust, action-oriented (although voluntary) document, highlighting a number of steps for the future survival of the biosphere. Over 30,000 people attended the parallel nongovernmental summit that took place in the center of Rio, geographically and ideologically removed from the uninspiring, formal government conference. The NGO space was a forest of white marquees galvanized by music, theater, debate, and a sense of hope, at least in the beginning. The largest marquee in the center of the park housed *La Planeta Femea*

New Directions for Adult and Continuing Education • DOI: 10.1002/ace

(The Female Planet), where hundreds of women strategized, communed, sang, danced, and shared global experiences. Importantly for the field of adult education, the UN chose ICAE to organize the environmental education marquee/event. The document produced by the ICAE, the *Treaty on Environmental Education for Sustainable Societies and Global Responsibility* (ICAE, 1991), reflected conversations from Stockholm about peace and human rights. The *Treaty* was also much stronger on gender and women's rights and global equity, recognizing the greater impact of environmental destruction on women worldwide. It also challenged the concept of development, replacing it with the terms sustainability and societies, and it argued for the need to view all forms of environmental education not as "neutral but ideological. It is a political act" (p. 2)—an emphasis that remains very much needed today.

Although the political outcome of Rio 92 was disappointing, that of the 1997 New York Rio+5 conference was even more so. Organized to assess the progress by world leaders, the conference mainly concluded that little, if any, progress had been made. Hampered by the insatiable quest for profit that is now the defining characteristic of global neoliberal market ideology, the language in both formal and nonformal documents was too compromised to be of any value (Rio+5, 1997). A slight crack appeared in this political armor in the 2002 Johannesburg United Nations Conference on Sustainable Development, where the word "sustainable" was reinscribed with a different vision and practice of development—one that is still very much on the drawing board. This was a signal of hope; it remains in play, remaining only in the making, and must be approached cautiously. So while this summit was a major setback in terms of commitments and new targets, as were many before it, it galvanized new dialogues and partnerships among civil societies and the private sector, with additional government resources attached to support efforts to implement sustainable development (United Nations, 2002).

Perhaps the most problematic United Nations gathering was the one on Climate Change in Copenhagen in 2009. Although all the countries recognized the science of human-induced climate change, there were no real commitments to reduce harmful emissions. In many ways, it became a violent clash between science—both independent and bought—in which a recurrent themed emerged: "the West and the rest." We saw this in Rio 92 in the tension between the West's refusal to address consumption and the rest's rebuff to discuss concerns around population (Clover, 1995). Again this tension emerged at Rio+20 (United Nations, 2012) around discussions of the green economy and the attempt to address sustainable development and the emergence of substantive differences in what this would mean to the West and to the rest, who had little (if any) economy, green or otherwise (Cianci, 2012; Watts, 2012). Equally problematic in Copenhagen, although seldom discussed, was the discursive construction of competing sciences—privileged knowledge was positioned as superior to the knowledge(s) of those experiencing the impacts of climate change. Secondly, it shifted the gaze to a single issue, away from the plethora of environmental problems. In our adult

New Directions for Adult and Continuing Education • DOI: 10.1002/ace

education work, we must never lose sight of the multiplicity of ecological problems that are so intimate and so violent in the lives of so many.

Environmental Education

Discussions at the conferences on environmental education outlined earlier were paralleled elsewhere. For example, in 1977 the UN organized an International Environmental Education Workshop in Belgrade. *The Belgrade Charter* outlined the gravity of the environmental situation and established education goals, objectives, target audiences, and guiding principles. While this document recognized the political edge required in education for change, its primary focus was on individual behavior modification, awareness raising, and education about the environment. It fell well short of identifying a more politically intensive program for education and learning for action, resulting in neutralizing, depoliticizing, and "science-izing" (if you will pardon this awkward neologism) public environmental education. This individual strategy towards environmental education prevailed at the subsequent conferences in Moscow (1987) and Thessaloniki (1997) despite efforts by activists and members of ICAE's Learning for Environmental Action Programme.

However, an encouraging change occurred at the Fourth International Environmental Conference held in Ahmedabad in 2007. Jointly organized by UNESCO and the United Nations Centre for Technical and Vocational Education (UNEVOC), this conference determinedly emphasized adult and nonformal education and repoliticized education to challenge the global greed paradigm and to work towards greater global "equity and social justice" (UNESCO/UNEVOC, 2007, pp. 1–2). In many ways these results were reminiscent of the Rio 92 *Treaty,* the *Hamburg Declaration*, and the documents produced by the ICAE for Rio+20.

The Forward March of Hamburg and the Setback at Belém

Environmental adult educators played a key role in the 1992 Rio Summit, as they also did in 1997 at CONFINTEA V. There, for the first time in the history of UN adult education conferences, the environment was treated equally with more familiar thematic areas such as literacy. Another major difference at CONFINTEA V from previous ones concerned civil society actors: nongovernmental organizations and voluntary agencies, adult education practitioners and scholars, and UN agency or program (e.g., UNESCO, UNEP, FAO) administrators and leaders all sat together in the thematic working groups as well as on the conference floor. The ability to lobby governments, however, does not mean that all recommendations found their way into official positions. However, even though the environmental areas of the *Hamburg Declaration* were compromised, they were nevertheless visionary. Ideas extended from using adult education activities to increase people's capacity to develop ecologically sustainable, innovative initiatives, to recognizing and integrating "indigenous and traditional knowledge of the interaction between human beings and nature into adult learning programs" (UNESCO, 1997, p. 22). They sought to ensure "the accountability of decision-makers in the context of policies relating to the environment, population and development" (p. 22) to enabling both women and others to exercise their human rights, including reproductive and sexual health rights. The latter not only raised support for women's global struggle against powerful anti-choice ideology, legislation and religious sentiment, but it also fulfilled a potential to wrestle "with issues surrounding sexual minorities" (Hill, 2007, p. 1).

CONFINTEA V had rendered visible and emphasized the environment, but the concept received little mention at CONFINTEA VI. The preamble to the *Belém Framework* (UNESCO Institute for Lifelong Learning, 2009) noted that education enabled youth and adults "*to cope* with . . . *climate change*" (p. 18; emphasis ours) and included a vague reference to *environmental development*. While we are unclear what this latter phrase means, it smacks of the seemingly unshakeable sustainable development discourse. Of course, neither CONFINTEA conference challenged the hegemony of unbridled capitalism. However, there were two advances in Belém: the acknowledgment of the gender-specific disproportionately negative impact of a carbon-saturated planet on women and the inclusion of youth in the document. While many adult educators have an aversion to youth—it is only millimeters from the all-consuming discourse of schools—the environment is certainly an issue and preoccupation of young people, especially young activists (Clover & Shaw, 2009; Walter, 2009).

Plus Ça Change . . . : Rio+20 and Beyond

Turning briefly to Rio+20, adult educators, alongside thousands of environmental activists, reentered the global environmental policy battlefield. As adult educators continued to dialogue in a quest for new language and ways forward, they attempted to reinsert the environment within the discourse of human rights. In the end, however, the official document, *The Future We Want* (United Nations, 2012), only enshrined a statement "recalling" *The Stockholm Declaration* and acknowledging and reaffirming a host of others. Yet one statement in particular is worth mentioning in its entirety:

> We are *determined to reinvigorate political will and to raise the level of commitment* by the international community to move the sustainable development agenda forward, through the achievement of the internationally agreed development goals, including the Millennium Development Goals. We further reaffirm our respective *commitments to other relevant internationally* agreed goals in the economic, social and environmental fields since 1992. We therefore resolve *to take concrete measures* that accelerate implementation of sustainable development commitments. (para. 18; emphasis ours)

New Directions for Adult and Continuing Education • DOI: 10.1002/ace

Despite sleight-of-hand words (such as relevant), this statement speaks of "concrete goals" and demonstrates that governments of the world are not simply a unified, ecologically myopic mass. There were also other promising signs, including the emphasis on indigenous peoples and pastorals and the potential of their knowledge, leadership of women, and a renewed focus on youth and public-private partnerships. Trade unions were mentioned for the first time ever, and there was an attempt to reorient the term "sustainable development."

The document fell short in not directly mentioning adult education and referring to nonformal learning only once. The Chinese government even questioned its relevance to "real" education (that is, schools), fearing a well-informed citizenry. But the document is peppered with such familiar terms as training, capacity building, active participation, information sharing, empowerment, knowledge enhancement, and other phrases directly related to the aims of environmental adult education. One of the more interesting developments at Rio+20 was the first production of a *People's Sustainability Treaty on Higher Education* (2011). Although higher education had been one concern at CONFINTEA V (but not VI), the topic was in no way related to the environment. But the *Treaty* called for universities to transform themselves in terms recognizing that:

> Sustainable development is itself a learning process. Achieving progress requires [universities and colleges] to build capacity, learn through experience and collaboration. Implementing change towards sustainable development . . . requires the creation of opportunities to co-construct knowledge and develop competencies of staff and students along the journey. (p. 3)

Educative Activism

Unfortunately, the various Frameworks or Agendas for Action have produced little or no headway on the political front. Both CONFINTEA V and VI were soft on requisite approaches to solving contemporary environmental crises, which demand an informed and active citizenry and a strong civil society. Indeed, by UNESCO's own admissions, the 2010 target for conserving biodiversity, defending habitats of threatened species, making improvements to unsanitary slum conditions, and addressing a host of other commitments has been missed. Clearly, if the actions proposed in 1972 had been taken, we would not have required the endless parade of conferences and documents. But they were not.

But let us reiterate that although all is not well, neither is all lost. To see only the negative in the previous canvas is to throw up ones hands in despair. That is neither a principle of environmental adult education nor a respectful attitude for the literally hundreds of initiatives taken around the world by those who refuse to believe that all is lost. Even as neoliberalism and capitalism generate and sustain acute environmental problems, positive, unrelenting forces emanate from defiant activists and educative imaginations. People are intervening, persevering, critically and creatively seeking social and environmental redress, and giving credence to alternative realities. Indeed, Walter (2009) believes adult education is "well-positioned to lead the way forward in fostering environmental awareness and action amongst adults, social institutions and social movements" (p. 3). We need to recognize environmental adult education in its multiplicity, variance, breadth, and scope.

The "New Education"—Environment, Health, and Population

The history of UN—including UNESCO—direct involvement in issues of population and health is equally as complex as that for the environment. The document *Promoting the Quality and Pertinence of Education—Global Challenges, New Educations* (UNESCO, n.d.) lists 20 UN programs, actions, or conferences on population alone, beginning in 1965. In that year, UN Secretary-General U. Thant warned that, owing to population growth, we were at a turning point that would lead to disease, starvation, and social collapse. Since his distress signal, the UN has been a driving force in building new educations: environmental education, population education, and health education.

The UN states that in 2010, the world's population reached 6.9 billion persons, with projections of 9.3 billion by 2050 and more than 10 billion by the century's end. The document *Urban Population, Development and the Environment 2011* (UNESCO, 2011) is unambiguous about the intersections of population, health (for example, sanitation and disease), and ecosystems (climate change, toxic particles in the air, energy consumption and the effects on human health). Woefully, as has been illustrated earlier for the environment, tragic situations and necessary actions now were foreseen but ignored decades earlier. For example, in 1994 the International Conference on Population and Development adopted a program for action that advocated the integration of population demographics into environmental assessment and sustainable development decisions. Thus, whether the subject is environment, population, or health, the records show ebbs and flows of pledges made, actions demanded, and behaviors advocated with only limited success when compared to the gargantuan issues at hand.

Ways Forward

While there are many ways we could move forward, here we outline only three. First, adult educators can link themselves to protest activities, finding ways to connect with other organizations and groups and to enter the struggle. A plethora of creative environmental adult educative activism is taking place with and through various media, including the arts such as popular theater, quilting, music, and puppetry (Branagan, 2005; Clover & Shaw,

2009; Walter, 2009). Researchers identify a "multiplicity of approaches from reformist demands on elites to revolutionary challenges to dominant paradigms, challenges aimed at fundamentally different human/environment relations" (Branagan, 2005, p. 35). The list is seemingly endless; the point is that there is no shortage of ways forward.

Second, documents from various conferences can be adopted as teaching resources. They provide a firsthand and critical platform for debate and ways to generate new ideas. They become tools for literacy. Indeed, the *Belém Framework for Action* (UNESCO Institute for Lifelong Learning, 2009) affirms that literacy is the most significant foundation for a comprehensive, inclusive, and integrated approach to lifelong and lifewide learning. This surely includes environmental literacy (known as ecolacy) as well as health and population literacy. The concept of ecolacy is rich in that it filters environmental knowledge in a way that seeks understanding coupled with the question "Then what?" Ecological and environmental literacy mean going beyond single (and simple) answers to further questions. These enable exploration of the impacts of complex, intricately interconnected systems, including nature's feedback loops, and the eco-ethical dimensions of choices.

Third, the United Nations Fourth World Conference on Women in Beijing (United Nations, 1995) preceded CONFINTEA V by two years. It clearly states that continuing environmental degradation, though affecting all human life, often has the most direct impact on women, as noted earlier. The Beijing *Framework for Action* clearly links women's health with an ecologically devastated environment. As ecological crises persist and grow, the empowerment of women is a fundamental requirement for change and security. Adult educators must continue to encourage their governments to undertake strategic actions to remediate gender inequalities in the management of natural resources and in safeguarding the environment. One would hope that surely these tenets would have surfaced profoundly in 1997 in the Hamburg conference. But it appears that the distance from Beijing to Hamburg was too great to travel in the two years that separated the two conferences. The ensuing decade and half seems to have been equally nonnavigable. Looking at the distant horizon, the question remains whether adult educators will have the courage and vision to sail the rough ecological and political seas that inevitably lie ahead.

References

Alfred, M. (Ed.). (2011). *Adult Learning, 22*(4).

Amnesty International. (2012). *Rio+20 outcome document undermined by human rights opponents*. Retrieved from http://www.amnesty.org/en/news/rio20-outcome-document-under mined-human-rights-opponents-2012-06-22

Branagan, M. (2005). Environmental adult education, activism and the arts. *Convergence, 38*(4), 33–50.

Cianci, M. (2012). *Ningún país se quiere mostrar poco cordial con las corporaciones [No country wants to be shown to be too friendly with corporations].* Retrieved from http://www.campanaderechoeducacion.org/participacion/?p=678

Clover, D. E. (1995). Learning for environmental action: Building international consensus. In B. Cassara (Ed.), *Adult education through world collaboration* (pp. 219–230). Malabar, FL: Krieger.

Clover, D. E. (1999). *Learning patterns of landscape and life: Towards a learning framework for environmental adult education* (Unpublished doctoral dissertation). University of Toronto, Toronto, Canada.

Clover, D. E. (2011). "You've Got the Power": Documentary film as a tool of environmental adult education. *Journal of Adult and Continuing Education, 17*(2), 20–36.

Clover, D. E., & Shaw, K. (2009). Re-imagining consumption: Political and creative practices of arts-based environmental adult education. In J. Sandlin & P. McLaren (Eds.), *Critical pedagogies of consumption: Living and learning in the shadow of the "Shopocalypse"* (pp. 203–213). New York, NY: Routledge.

Hill, R. J. (2007). Finding a voice for sexual minority rights (lesbian, gay, bisexual, transgender, indigenous/Two-Spirit, and Queer): Some comprehensive policy considerations. *Convergence, 40*(3/4), 169–180.

Hill, R. J., Daigle, E. A., Graybeal, L., Walker, W., Avalon, C., Fowler, N., & Massey, M. W. (2008). *A review and critique of the 2008 United States National Report on the Development and State of the Art of Adult Learning and Education (ALE).* Report to the International Council for Adult Education Virtual CONFINTEA VI Seminar.

International Council for Adult Education (ICAE). (1991). *Treaty on environmental education for sustainable societies and global responsibility.* Toronto, Canada: Author.

Kushner, J. (2009). Wangari Maathai: Righteous leader of environmental and social change. In *Proceedings of the 50th Annual Adult Education Research Conference* (pp. 195–200). Chicago, IL: National Louis University.

People's Sustainability Treaty on Higher Education. (2011). Retrieved from http://www.uncsd2012.org/index.php?page=view&type=1006&menu=153&nr=135

Rio+5. (1997). *United Nations Earth Summit+5.* Retrieved from http://www.un.org/esa/earthsummit/

UNESCO. (n.d.). *Promoting the quality and pertinence of education—global challenges, new educations.* Retrieved from http://www.unesco.org/education/educprog/50y/brochure/promotin/210.htm

UNESCO. (1997). *The Hamburg Declaration on adult learning and agenda for the future.* Paris, France: Author.

UNESCO. (2011). *Urban population, development and the environment 2011.* Retrieved from http://www.un.org/esa/population/publications/2011 UrbanPopDevEnv_Chart/urban_wallchart_2011-web-smaller.pdf

UNESCO Institute for Lifelong Learning. (2009). *Harnessing the power and potential of adult learning and education for a viable future: Belém framework for action.* Hamburg, Germany: Author.

UNESCO/UNEVOC. (2007, November). *Moving forward from Ahmedabad . . . Environmental education in the 21st Century.* Paper presented at the 4th International Conference on Environmental Education CEE, Ahmedabad, India. Retrieved from http://www.tbilisiplus30.org/Final%20Recommendations.pdf

United Nations. (1972). *Stockholm declaration of the United Nations conference on the human environment.* Retrieved from http://www.unep.org/Documents.Multilingual/Default.asp?documentid=97&articleid=1503

United Nations. (1992, June). *Agenda 21.* Presented at the UN Conference on Environment and Development (UNCED), Rio de Janeiro, Brazil. Retrieved from http://habitat.igc.org/agenda21/

United Nations. (1995). *Fourth World Conference on Women, Beijing, China—Action for Equality, Development and Peace. Platform for Action.* Retrieved from http://www.un.org/womenwatch/daw/beijing/platform/plat1.htm

United Nations. (2002). *World Summit on Sustainability. Johannesburg, South Africa.* Retrieved from http://www.rrcap.ait.asia/wssd/Political%20declaration_4%20Sep%2002.pdf

United Nations. (2012). *The future we want.* New York, NY: Author.

Walter, P. (2009). Philosophies of adult environmental education. *Adult Education Quarterly, 60*(1), 3–25.

Watts, J. (2012, June 19). Rio+20: Anger and Dismay at Weakened Draft Agreement. *The Guardian.* Retrieved from http://www.guardian.co.uk/environment/2012/jun/19/rio-20-weakened-draft-agreement

DARLENE E. CLOVER is a professor in leadership studies, faculty of education, University of Victoria, Canada. She co-organized the environmental education tent at Rio 1992 and coined the term "environmental adult education."

ROBERT HILL is an associate professor of adult education at the University of Georgia, Athens, Georgia.

New Directions for Adult and Continuing Education • DOI: 10.1002/ace

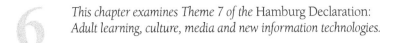

This chapter examines Theme 7 of the Hamburg Declaration: *Adult learning, culture, media and new information technologies.*

Adult Learning and the Promise of New Technologies

Dejan Dinevski, Marko Radovan

Theme 7 of the *Hamburg Declaration on Adult Learning and Agenda for the Future* (UNESCO, 1997) suggested promoting adult learning through the development of media learning and fostering the use of new technologies. It recognized distance and online learning as key factors for widening worldwide access to adult education. The *Declaration* also called for the revision of copyright and patenting regulations to promote the distribution of learning materials and for strengthening the role of libraries and other cultural institutions (museums, theaters, ecological parks, and others) as lifelong learning resources. Cultural institutions need not merely collect and preserve cultural artifacts and patterns but can also promote lifelong learning in communities. The *Hamburg Declaration* stressed that one of the most important tasks of adult education was the need to deepen knowledge of people's own cultures and to develop mutual understanding between cultures. Adult learners should be able to access all cultural institutions and use mass media and new technologies to create interactive communication and to build understanding and cooperation, especially as mass media is particularly important for political socialization and raising cultural awareness (Brookfield, 1986). In this chapter we examine the challenges and possibilities of digital technologies in promoting such access, supporting adult learning and fostering the interaction of adults with those from other cultures and society in general.

The Digital Age and (In)equality of Participation

The *Hamburg Declaration* stressed that new media and new technologies for learning should help all adults participate in learning. To what extent has this optimistic objective been achieved? Has the development of digital technologies

NEW DIRECTIONS FOR ADULT AND CONTINUING EDUCATION, no. 138, Summer 2013 © 2013 Wiley Periodicals, Inc.
Published online in Wiley Online Library (wileyonlinelibrary.com) • DOI: 10.1002/ace.20054
61

fulfilled the expectations of adult educators? We can observe a tremendous amount of development of digital technologies and the possibilities that they offer both as a part of our everyday lives or as tools for online teaching and learning. Digital technologies offer exceptionally promising tools to assist learning in general. They can change the ways we learn (when, where, and how) and can make learning more democratic and accessible. The use of media and information and communication technologies (ICTs) in widening access to adult learning can develop in many directions.

ICTs and the Internet are changing all aspects of life and functioning of society. Online learning in the developed world is expanding and becoming an important method of teaching and learning, although in many cases its use in learning processes is partial and uneven. Online materials and tools can also promote political, economic, or social debate, and online forums can give voice to previously ignored groups. On the other hand, if we want to achieve some of the goals stated in the *Hamburg Declaration*, we must not forget that learners must first have access to these tools and be able to use them. So, new digital technologies can also be a source of creating new inequalities and extending the marginalization of certain social groups. Progress in Western societies in this regard has been significant, but what about the rest of the world?

Widening access to learning or education and overall participation in society via new media and technologies can be realized only through the broad penetration of web-enabled devices (traditional and mobile). This is difficult to achieve at a global level, because only a small percentage of the world's population uses the Internet or has access to the World Wide Web. In fact, the majority of Internet usage comes from Western countries in North America, Oceania/Australia and Europe (Internet World Stats, 2011). Although access to online services overall has improved, the divide between different parts of the world is still immense. For example, developing countries have increased their share of the world's total number of Internet users from 44% in 2006 to 62% in 2011. Currently China has the fastest-growing group of Internet users: almost 25% of the world total and 37% of those from developing countries.

A more worrying gap can be seen if we look at demographics. The International Telecommunication Union reports that 45% of the world's Internet users in 2011 were younger than 25 (International Telecommunication Union, 2011). This group is the most underprivileged in developing countries, in which 70% of those under the age of 25 are not using the Internet, compared with 23% in developed countries (International Telecommunication Union, 2011). The share in developing countries could be vastly improved if school enrollment rates in developing countries increased and if schools were equipped with proper infrastructure. This problem has captured the attention of the OECD (2001), which recognized that ICT could enlarge social differences in societies rather than close them unless specific policy interventions were undertaken.

Different Dimensions of the Digital Divide

It is commonly understood that adult learners who do not have access to digital technologies are becoming increasingly disadvantaged in the information age (Hayes, 2007) and such inequality has been described as a "digital divide" (Castells, 2002, p. 248; Van Dijk, 2005, p. 178). Researchers regard access as a prerequisite for overcoming inequality in a society in which dominant functions and social groups are increasingly organized around the Internet. This divide is mostly related to low economic status, low levels of educational attainment, and other social indicators that characterize social disadvantage, understood as a cause and consequence of digital illiteracy. According to Van Dijk (2005), developed countries are already closing the gap in terms of physical access to computers and the Internet, but in developing societies the gap is growing. In terms of the skill levels required to use digital technologies, the digital divide is also increasing. Van Dijk also believes that "information skills" (those needed for accessing, selecting, and processing information on the computer and the Internet) and "strategic skills" (the ability to use these resources to achieve specific goals) are still unevenly distributed in developed societies, but even more so in developing societies.

Other researchers have also claimed that access to digital technologies and the use of those technologies are important as contributors to social inequality (Hargittai & Walejko, 2008; Mossberger, Tolbert, & Stansbury, 2003; Warschauer, 2004). For example, in their paper about the creative activity and sharing of younger adults in the age of the Internet, Hargittai and Walejko (2008) explore online engagement. Their findings suggest that despite all the opportunities that online technologies and tools offer to Internet users, relatively few people take advantage of them. They also found that both creating and sharing are tied to people's socioeconomic status (as measured by their parents' education). This is especially true for content creation; for content sharing, Internet user skills were also an important influence on behavior. This suggests that merely providing access to digital technologies will not guarantee that those technologies are necessarily used in meaningful ways. In the next section, we will examine how such technologies might be included in educational settings and what challenges their presence represents for teaching and learning.

Impact of New Technologies on Teaching and Learning

The use of new information and communication technologies (ICT) in learning and teaching is commonly known as "e-learning". Although the data in previous sections show discrepancies in Internet access, e-learning in developed countries has witnessed an unprecedented expansion at all levels and modes of education in the last decade. It has created new didactical concepts and new opportunities to easily access the knowledge. Support for ICT has also resulted in more effective organization of learning processes.

New Directions for Adult and Continuing Education • DOI: 10.1002/ace

Of course, we cannot expect effective learning to take place just because we have perpetual and direct access to vast Internet resources and the knowledge they contain. In fact, ICTs can have a negative effect on users' learning capacity. But with the right preparation of electronic learning material and proper guidance, the Internet and its related technology can enhance learning. The Internet and e-learning are still in their early stages of development, and in the quest for optimal educational application one has to be aware of both sides—their strengths and opportunities as well as their weaknesses and threats.

Strengths and Opportunities of e-Learning for Adults

If we can overcome the barriers to access resulting from digital divides, e-learning has the obvious potential to make adult learning more effective, efficient, and pervasive. For adult education, its major strength is that it provides greater flexibility regarding time, space, pace, content, and methods of learning. The basic mode of content delivery in e-learning is accessing the learning objects (being in a variety of media formats) in a virtual learning environment (VLE). VLEs offer tools that allow teachers to give online lectures and learners to follow courses using the electronic learning material and to do experiments in virtual laboratories. Learning objects also let teachers and learners (re)use and (re)arrange learning materials in different orders—thereby creating different courses or course units. This is particularly suitable for adult learners, because it can provide appropriate levels of content to students with different levels of background knowledge.

The quality of e-learning for adults depends not only on products, such as learning content, or services, but also on the interactions of the learner with the contents, tasks, tutors, and other learners. Recently e-learning has seen the wide use of the Web 2.0 technologies (the Internet as a platform for information sharing, interoperability, user-centered design, and collaboration), which has resulted in some major changes in these interactions, particularly the development of didactic concepts characterized by the term "collaborative learning." Collaborative learning is one of the major didactical opportunities of adult learners, because it explicitly supports creation, collaboration, and communication. Initially defined by Beckman (1990), the concept had been researched before: Collier (1980) used the term "peer-group learning," Cooper (1990) called it "cooperative learning," and Fiechtner and Davis (1992) used the term "learning groups." Common to all these studies was a framework of meticulously planned and engaged organizing of groups (the formation of groups containing a small number of participants), supporting the groups in the planning and performance of group work, the preparation of instructions for group work, reviews of group work, help with uncooperative members, and other areas.

Collaboration in a social media environment is not limited to a certain place, a particular time, or a small number of participants. Collaboration is considered as any process of working with others and having a common objective. The collaboration tools that are available for supporting and promoting participative behavior are not sufficient for the group to learn. In a search for the concept of collaborative learning in the social media environment Freire (2000), Garrison, Anderson, and Archer (2000), and Wells (1999) argued that critical discourse is important within collaborative learning environments. Indeed, in his book on the culture of collaboration, Rosen (2007) proposes 10 cultural elements that support value creation: trust, sharing, goals, innovation, environment, collaborative chaos, constructive confrontation, communication, community, and value. Because the collaboration culture requires a developed personality that is capable of critical reflection and has wide-ranging social and communication skills, the collaborative learning concept is particularly suitable for adult education. Further development of collaborative learning is based on the connectivist theory of learning (Ally, 2008), which views knowledge as existing within systems that are accessed through people participating in activities.

Widening Access to Educational Resources

For adult learners in developed countries and for those who have the basic digital literacy skills and Internet connection, a key issue is access to high quality learning materials. The Open Educational Resources (OER) movement, promoted by UNESCO, is addressing this issue. OER, according to UNESCO, refers to "the open provision of educational resources, enabled by information and communication technologies for consultation, use and adaptation by a community of users for non-commercial purposes" (UNESCO, 2002, p. 24). The provision of OER presents a broader political and social challenge, because OER does not generate profit directly. Hylén (2006) explores five incentives to become involved as a provider of OERs: sharing knowledge is beneficial; it increases the value of existing investments of public money; it can cut costs and improve quality; it can be good for public relations; and it provides a chance to explore new global business models. According to Gesser (2007), OERs also have the following core attributes:

- Access to open content (including metadata) is provided free of charge for educational institutions, content services, and the end-users such as teachers, students, and lifelong learners;
- Content is liberally licensed for re-use in educational activities, generally free from restrictions on modifying, combining, and repurposing the content; consequently, the content should ideally be designed for easy re-use in that open content standards and formats are being employed;
- Educational systems and tools software is used for which the source code is available (that is, open source software) and that there are open Application Programming Interfaces (open APIs) and authorizations to

re-use Web-based services as well as resources (for example, for educational content RSS feeds).

It is noteworthy that pedagogical models are not regarded as key for OERs. Instead, technical and management considerations rather than the perspectives of educational practitioners have tended to dominate discussions. However, to achieve the goal of efficient adult learning experiences, didactics and pedagogy must also be considered in the search for practical solutions.

Copyright Issues of Online Learning

One important issue mentioned in the *Hamburg Declaration* is the promotion of the fair use of intellectual property by "revising copyright and patenting regulations to promote the distribution of learning materials while preserving the rights of authors" (UNESCO, 1997, p. 24). This area is very important in preparing learning materials for traditional classrooms, but it deals with an entirely new dimension when planning online learning. Copyright issues in modern societies are important because access to information is seen as an essential development resource. Here, the Internet plays a central role: it offers unprecedented media access to information and allows the use of this information in very different ways and for very different purposes. The wide availability and diversity of potential applications supported by ICT gives authors new and better opportunities for creating online learning materials. At the same time, there is an increased risk of the illegal use of a creation that lacks adequate protection, and authors (schools or teachers) can be penalized. Educational institutions or teachers have two options when using a copyrighted work: they can ask for permission from the copyright owner (often a difficult, time-consuming process), or they can use exceptions to the copyright law. Around the world copyright legislation is regulated by different domestic laws and international agreements, but in general a work is limited to use in the "analog" (nondigital) classroom.

There are two main directions for current legislation and efforts to protect digital content. First, technological measures and systems for digital rights management (DRM) are being developed that allow authors full control over the use of their works and can prevent any violation of the use of a particular digital work. Due to the need for total control over the use of a digital work, this approach requires control over distribution and over the computer equipment of each user. The problem of this approach is demonstrated in terms of privacy. Its restrictive nature can negatively impact the research and development of individual technologies and the development of e-content. A second direction was developed under the auspices of the Creative Commons (CC) organization (http://creativecommons.org), a nonprofit organization that offers licenses for authors that clearly define permissible and unauthorized uses of their works so that the works can freely be exchanged between users.

Weaknesses and Threats of Omnipresent Digital Technologies

So far we have explained how digital technologies could be used to enhance learning. In the early days of the Internet, the World Wide Web and electronic communication were perceived as an enhancement to everyday life—whether professional or personal. It clearly saved time, provided instant access to relevant information, and deepened communication. However, it is important to acknowledge that the same technologies can also distract users and impair the concentration and cognitive attention necessary for learning to take place. Also, unlimited or excessive use of digital technologies can pose a serious threat to the user.

What has changed from earlier times? Today people in developed societies seem to be constantly online, using numerous computer and mobile device channels for multitasking. Online, people can simultaneously text, chat, browse, share, post, tweet, shop, and prepare presentations. They can have multiple virtual selves, sometimes fully formed avatars, residing in the Internet. Not only does this change what people do, but it also changes how they relate to others. Sociologist Sherry Turkle (2011) claims that modern people are getting used to a new way of being alone together—people want to be with each other in the here and now, but at the same time they also want to be elsewhere, connected to different places and people. According to Turkle, pervasive use of the Internet and the emergence of constant mobile connectivity is resulting in increased alienation, lack of reflective communication, inability to focus, demand for quick and simplified answers, incapacity to grasp deeper concepts, and increasingly addictive behaviors.

Omnipresent digital technology is bringing major shifts into the very basics of our social life and cognitive tasks—some of which (such as memory, communication, writing and computing skills, or sense of direction) also extend to mobile devices. "Cyborg anthropologist" Amber Case, editor of the site www.cyborganthropology.com, goes further and questions if the online extension of the mental self means that we are slowly turning into cyborgs (organisms to which exogenous components have been added for the purpose of adapting to new environments). Focusing on learning, we can conclude that excessive use of digital technologies in everyday life can damage cognitive processes that are a prerequisite for learning to take place at all.

Conclusions

The goals of adult learning that were presented in Theme 7 of the *Hamburg Declaration* related to widening access to new learning technologies and the possibilities that these technologies might bring to learners and to providers of adult learning. Clearly, as the Belém report (UNESCO Institute for Lifelong Learning, 2009) identifies, significant progress has been made on realizing many of these goals. However, challenges still remain, particularly in developing digital literacy and widening access to online learning. In the *Hamburg Declaration*, adult education was charged with a prominent role in shaping the globalized world of the approaching 21st century. We agree with Duke and Hinzen (2011) that notions of literacy skills must be expanded beyond simply reading, writing, and numeracy to also include skills that are required to effectively use information technology. Such skills have become almost a prerequisite for daily life—people need them in their private life, at their work as well as for effective learning in general.

New technology can be harnessed to provide many learning opportunities to adults who cannot or have been unable to participate in formal education. It can also be an important basis for providing information, guidance, and counseling. A review of research related to access to the Internet and to the Internet as a learning tool for active participation in society, shows that there are still several challenges facing adult educators and policy makers.

However, our review reveals that adult educators take good advantage of learning tools that are offered by digital technologies. Online learning took big steps in the last decade. Much research recognizes the main qualities and opportunities of online learning as well as establishing what distinguishes e-learning from traditional approaches. Open questions still remain on how to integrate new technology in other, more traditional forms of education, how to improve interaction between learning content (objects), learners and their tutors, and how to train educational personnel to use online tools efficiently. We have shown, on the other hand, that overwhelming use of digital technologies in everyday life can pose a serious threat to the learning processes and also learning capacity of this special group of users.

Nevertheless the important long-term problem remains universal access to the Internet. All of the potentials of digital technologies that are mentioned in the *Hamburg Declaration* are useless if individuals cannot access them or lack necessary skills for their effective use. The data on access indicates large demographic and socio-economic gaps throughout the world. Unfortunately, there is no simple and quick solution. This remains an important challenge in the years to come, both for developed and developing countries.

References

Ally, M. (2008). Foundations of educational theory for online learning. In T. Anderson (Ed.), *The theory and practice of online learning* (pp. 15–44). Edmonton, Canada: Athabasca University Press.

Beckman, M. (1990). Collaborative learning: Preparation for the workplace and democracy. *College Teaching, 38*(4), 128–133.

Brookfield, S. (1986). Media power and the development of media literacy: An adult educational interpretation. *Harvard Educational Review, 56*(2), 151–171.

Castells, M. (2002). *The Internet galaxy.* Oxford, England: Oxford University Press.

Collier, K. G. (1980). Peer-group learning in higher education: The development of higher-order skills. *Studies in Higher Education, 5*(1), 55–62.

Cooper, J. (1990). Cooperative learning and college teaching: Tips from the trenches. *Teaching Professor, 4*(5), 1–2.

Duke, C., & Hinzen, H. (2011). Adult education and lifelong learning: Within UNESCO: CONFINTEA, Education for All, and beyond. *Adult Learning, 22*(4), 18–23.

Fiechtner, S. B., & Davis, E. A. (1992). Why some groups fail: A survey of students' experiences with learning groups. In A. Goodsell, M. Maher, V. Tinto, & Associates (Eds.), *Collaborative learning: A sourcebook for higher education* (pp. 86–98). University Park, PA: National Center on Postsecondary Teaching, Learning, and Assessment, Pennsylvania State University.

Freire, P. (2000). *Pedagogy of the oppressed*. New York, NY: Continuum.

Garrison, D. R., Anderson, T., & Archer, W. (2000). Critical inquiry in a text-based environment: Computer conferencing in higher education. *The Internet and Higher Education, 2*(2–3), 1–19.

Gesser, G. (Ed.). (2007). *Open educational practices and resources*. Salzburg, Austria: Open e-Learning Content Observatory Services.

Hargittai, E., & Walejko, G. (2008). The participation divide: Content creation and sharing in the digital age. *Information, Community and Society, 11*(2), 239–256.

Hayes, E. (2007). Reconceptualizing Adult Basic Education and the digital divide. In A. Belzer (Ed.), *Toward defining and improving quality in Adult Basic Education: Issues and challenges* (pp. 203–220). New York, NY: Lawrence Erlbaum.

Hylén, J. (2006, September). *Open educational resources: Opportunities and challenges*. Paper presented at Open Education 2006: Community, Culture & Content, Utah State University.

Internet World Stats. (2011). Retrieved from http://www.internetworldstats.com/stats.htm

International Telecommunication Union. (2011). *The world in 2011: ICT facts and figures*. Retrieved from http://www.itu.int/ITU-D/ict/facts/2011/index.html

Mossberger, K., Tolbert, C. J., & Stansbury, M. (2003). *Virtual inequality: Beyond the digital divide*. Washington, DC: Georgetown University Press.

OECD. (2001). *Understanding the digital divide*. Paris, France: Author.

Rosen, E. (2007). The culture of collaboration: Maximizing time, talent and tools to create value in the global economy. San Francisco, CA: Red Ape Publishing.

Turkle, S. (2011). *Alone together*. New York, NY: Basic Books.

UNESCO. (1997). *The Hamburg Declaration on adult learning and agenda for the future*. Paris, France: Author.

UNESCO. (2002). *Forum on the impact of open courseware for higher education in developing countries: Final report*. Paris, France: Author.

UNESCO Institute for Lifelong Learning. (2009). *Harnessing the power and potential of adult learning and education for a viable future: Belém framework for action*. Hamburg, Germany: Author.

Van Dijk, J. (2005). *The deepening divide: Inequality in the information society*. Thousand Oaks, CA: Sage.

Warschauer, M. (2004). *Technology and social inclusion: Rethinking the digital divide*. Boston, MA: MIT Press.

Wells, G. (1999). *Dialogic inquiry*. Cambridge, England: Cambridge University Press.

DEJAN DINEVSKI *is an associate professor in technology-enhanced learning in the faculties of education and medicine, University of Maribor, Slovenia. He has coordinated a number of national and international projects in the wider area of e-learning for different groups of adult learners.*

MARKO RADOVAN *is an assistant professor in the didactics of adult education in the faculty of arts, University of Ljubljana, Slovenia. His research mainly involves adult participation in education and motivation to learn.*

New Directions for Adult and Continuing Education • DOI: 10.1002/ace

This chapter addresses Themes 8 and 10 of the Hamburg Declaration: *Adult learning for all: The rights and aspirations of different groups, and Enhancing international cooperation and solidarity.*

The Gap Between Aspiration and Practice

Alan Tuckett

At the time of the fifth UNESCO international conference on adult education (CONFINTEA V) in Hamburg in 1997, it seemed that a resilient alliance of governments and civil society organizations had been created. This alliance would have the commitment and cooperation needed to pursue the ambitious aspirations captured in the 10 themes of the *Hamburg Declaration on Adult Learning and Agenda for the Future* (UNESCO, 1997) adopted at the conference. In this chapter I explore what happened to the alliance and to the energy and confidence generated by the process in respect of two of the themes in the *Declaration*. Theme 8 concerned the rights and aspirations of different groups: the aged, migrants, gypsies and other nonterritorial and/or nomadic peoples, refugees, disabled people, and prison inmates; Theme 10 addressed increasing international cooperation and solidarity to enhance adult learning opportunities:

> International co-operation and solidarity must strengthen a new vision of adult learning which is both holistic, to embrace all aspects of life, and cross-sectoral, to include all areas of cultural, social and economic activity. (UNESCO, 1997, para. 50)

It is a story of the interplay of two visions of lifelong learning: one vision grounded in human rights and focused on inclusiveness, both essential for the expansion of equal access and achievement; the other vision focused on learning useful for the labor market as a key component in human capital, itself central to economic growth. The first vision has been promoted by UNESCO, the other by the Organisation for Economic Cooperation and Development (OECD), the International Monetary Fund (IMF), and World Bank.

NEW DIRECTIONS FOR ADULT AND CONTINUING EDUCATION, no. 138, Summer 2013 © 2013 Wiley Periodicals, Inc.
Published online in Wiley Online Library (wileyonlinelibrary.com) • DOI: 10.1002/ace.20055

The CONFINTEA V conference came towards the end of a decade that began with Jacques Delors arguing in the EC White Paper on Competitiveness and Employment (Commission of the European Communities, 1993) that lifelong learning was essential to foster both economic competitiveness and social cohesion. In 1996, as chair of the UNESCO Commission on Lifelong Learning, he published *Learning: The Treasure Within* (Delors, 1996), which highlighted four pillars of lifelong learning—learning to know, learning to do, learning to be, and learning to live together. At the same time, the OECD finance ministers became convinced that economic prosperity for industrial societies required strengthened human capital and that the pace of technological change necessitated the adoption of lifelong learning strategies. Meanwhile, through a succession of Presidency conferences engaging state and non-state actors, the European Union (EU) was laying the groundwork for its own lifelong learning strategy, adopted as part of its Lisbon Strategy that committed the EU states to raise participation rates in adult learning (EU, 2000).

Starting in the 1990s there had been a sequence of United Nations conferences: the Education for All conference in Jomtien (Thailand) in 1990, the Earth Summit in Rio de Janeiro in 1992, the Population conference in Cairo in 1994, the Beijing Women's Conference of 1995, CONFINTEA V itself in 1997, and the 2001 Durban conference against racism, racial discrimination, xenophobia, and other forms of discrimination. Each had identified learning challenges confronting the adult populations of the world in attempts to overcome poverty and want. CONFINTEA V had captured the spirit of those events by recognizing that adult learning is not just a good in itself but also a key catalyst for achieving a wide range of other social policy goals.

However, a by-product of the sequence of global conferences was that governments made a series of commitments at each event, far beyond the ability of all but the most affluent to finance and organize their implementation, at least without major investment from donor agencies and development partners. The growing recognition that the vision articulated in the 1990s conferences needed to be brought together led to the adoption at the UN Millennium Development Conference of a vision statement, from which eight key themes were expressed as Millennium Development Goals (MDG), intended to highlight key tasks in eradicating global poverty. In the same year UNESCO convened the Dakar recall conference on Education for All in 2000. The conference adopted Education for All targets which spanned the education for development needs of adults throughout the life-span. These included adult literacy, the promotion of participation for youth and adult learning, and the promotion of gender equality (UNESCO, 2000; United Nations [UN], 2000a, 2000b).

At one level, this could be seen as an early indication of success in meeting the aspirations outlined earlier in paragraph 50 of the *Hamburg Declaration*. To have a major impact on the prevalence of HIV/AIDS, on improved sanitation and clean water, or on effective strategies to live sustainably within the limits of the Earth's resources requires the imaginative understanding and agency of the adult populations affected by these policies. Thus, it might be expected that the role of adult learning (whether formal, nonformal, or informal) would be central to international cooperation in achieving the MDG. However, adult learning was not explicitly included in the distillation of the millennium vision statement in the Millennium Development Goals. Indeed, the only goals with a focus on education were the commitment to secure universal primary school access and to address the gender imbalance in access to education.

Multilateral and donor countries adopted the priorities articulated in the MDG with enthusiasm. The World Bank and UNESCO's Fast Track initiative, which focused on achieving universal primary education and delivered multilateral aid, reinforced this process. Country plans focused, too, on the headline tasks identified in the goals. As UN Secretary-General Ban-Ki Moon noted in the foreword to the Millennium Development Goals Report 2011, the goals "have raised awareness and shaped a broad vision that remains the overarching framework for the development activities of the United Nations" (UN, 2011, p. 3). But while this highlighted the breadth of the vision, in practice the targets have acted to narrow the focus of development—often to the detriment of adult learning opportunities.

At a recent meeting of the UNESCO National Commission in the UK, a senior official of the UK Department for International Development argued that the Millennium Development Goals had been more effective than any earlier initiatives in securing coherent international cooperation and focusing on major priorities in development. He pointed to improvements in access to clean water and schooling, as well as to reductions in the number of deaths of women in childbirth. Undoubtedly there have been positive educational developments in primary school participation and in girls' access to schooling. Yet the concentration of international and multilateral development funding on the eight Millennium Development Goals has come at a price for those Education for All targets not included in the MDG.

For adult education in particular, the focus on the MDG targets led to a diminution of international cooperation that involved state and non-state bodies working together. However, the adoption of development targets that omitted explicit reference to adult learning was not the sole reason for weakening international cooperation in the years following CONFINTEA V. The consolidation of neoliberal economic and social policies in much of the industrialized world was hard to square with the humanistic approach of the *Hamburg Declaration*. The impact of increased globalization of trade and services led, in much of the industrialized world, to limiting post-school educational investment to a narrow and immediately utilitarian curriculum. In addition, the onset of major international conflicts diverted resources from the development agenda in many countries. In short, both countries from the north and south were less and less inclined to make broadly-based adult learning a priority.

New Directions for Adult and Continuing Education • DOI: 10.1002/ace

At the same time the UNESCO Institute for Education faced a period of uncertainty during which its status within the UNESCO family of institutes, its funding, and its priorities came under sustained scrutiny. There were perhaps two further reasons for a weakening of state and civil society cooperation in addressing the *Hamburg Declaration*. Firstly, a number of governments working through the UN process concluded that the 1990s conferences had given too much prominence to the voices of civil society, and that this had an impact on the range and achievability of the targets adopted. But secondly, many civil society bodies expressed increasing frustration at the growth of a neoliberal consensus in international discourse and determined to identify strategies necessary to create a world in which everyone could live secure and fulfilling lives.

In 2001 civil society organizations meeting in Porto Alegre in Brazil created the World Social Forum. This extraordinary and energetic coming together of tens of thousands of activists were united in the belief that "another world is possible" and were determined to explore how it might be achieved. Although the Forum did not adopt platforms, it did energize in civil society activity, and led to an annual global festival as well as regional and national forums, of activist learning. In its distinctive way, the Forum contributes to the *Hamburg Declaration*'s vision, offering a platform for the voices of indigenous and landless people, for disabled people, and others excluded from dominant discourses (International Council for Adult Education [ICAE], 2004).

However, despite Porto Alegre, for those priority groups identified in Theme 8 of *Hamburg Declaration*, the comparative weakening of the alliance between governments and civil society actors in lifelong learning was, overall, bad news. The commitment to social solidarity had opened with a reassertion that the right to education is a universal right, and includes all people. It continued:

> While there is agreement that adult learning must be accessible to all, the reality is that many groups are still excluded, such as the aged, migrants, gypsies and other non-territorial and/or nomadic peoples, refugees, disabled people and prison inmates. These groups should have access to education programmes that accommodate them within an individual-centred pedagogy capable of meeting their needs and facilitating their full participation in society. All members of the community should be invited and, where necessary, assisted in participating in adult learning. This implies meeting a diversity of learning needs. (UNESCO, 1997, para. 43)

The *Global Report on Adult Learning and Education* (GRALE) found that effective outreach and engagement for many excluded groups relied on the engagement of civil society agencies, backed by state resources—"since the capacity for flexibility and vitality of such practitioners has been shown to be successful in targeting disadvantaged and rural populations" (UNESCO Institute for Lifelong Learning [UIL], 2009, p. 71).

As a result of these changes in the external policy climate, by the time of the CONFINTEA V midterm review conference in 2003 in Bangkok, much of the optimism generated in Hamburg had evaporated. A measure of the marginalization of the adult education agenda was that there were more non-state actors than representatives of member states. And Sir John Daniel, then the UNESCO Assistant General Secretary for Education, told the conference that despite their claims for the potential of adult education to promote liberty, justice, and peace, adult educators had the reputation for being "boring, sanctimonious, backward looking, and parentalist" (Daniel, 2003, p. 3)—scarcely qualities, he argued, likely to influence governments. "Can we point," he asked, "to examples where adult education has helped to prevent wars? Has adult education ever made a terrorist pause on his way to plant a bomb?" (p. 3). This was a startlingly different perspective from that of UNESCO or its participating states in 1997, which reflected the shift in international discourse that followed increased anxiety about terrorism and security in the years following September 11, 2001. It was also curiously blind to exactly that evidence generated by the Centre for Reseach on the Wider Benefits of Learning in London—work subsequently built on in a succession of OECD studies—which demonstrated that engagement in adult learning increases trust and tolerance (OECD, 2007; Preston & Green, 2003; Schuller, Preston, Hammond, Brassett-Grundy, & Bynner, 2004).

At the Bangkok conference, ICAE published a monitoring report on progress towards the achievement of the commitments entered into by governments at Hamburg in a sample of 20 countries, which were chosen to reflect the full range of development as measured by the Human Development Index (ICAE, 2003). It made for depressing reading. Far from reporting significant progress, it showed that there had been retrenchment and a reduction of adult learning opportunities in a significant majority of countries studied. Further, this reduction had affected most severely exactly those groups that the *Hamburg Declaration* had recognized as in need of specific attention. The report identified a worldwide commitment to equal opportunities in principle, but its practice was somewhat different:

> Around the world, it is clear that simply stating that equal opportunities exist for all does not ensure equal participation from all. This is so because complex patterns of discrimination act as powerful obstacles to access. These patterns act both through cultural messages given by society and through personal subordinated attitudes. Therefore if educational opportunities are to reach all groups which are discriminated against, then specific obstacles to access must be identified and programmes organised in response to them. (pp. 16–17)

Alas, though it was able to point to encouraging developments in specific countries, the report found little systematic evidence that such programs abounded.

New Directions for Adult and Continuing Education • DOI: 10.1002/ace

By the time of CONFINTEA VI in 2009, the picture for marginalized groups had not changed significantly. The GRALE report noted that "disadvantaged adults, especially those with multiple disadvantages, are least likely to participate in adult education" (UIL, 2009, p. 71). The report documented low levels of participation and social inequalities in access to and participation in adult education. It noted that this derived from a twin problem: first, the need to secure the policies and resources required to address underrepresentation; second, the need to motivate adults from disadvantaged groups to understand the benefits of participation.

For each of the groups identified in Theme 8 of the *Hamburg Declaration*, the GRALE report describes modest progress and major challenges. It notes, for example, an increase in industrialized countries' interests in engaging older people in learning—both to prolong working lives and to enhance active citizenship in rapidly aging societies. While Thailand targets adults over 60 as a priority for its programs, Help Age Ghana is designed to increase the participation of older people. Across Europe and North America Elderhostels and Universities of the Third Age provide evidence of older adults' self-help initiatives in securing learning opportunities. Nevertheless older people remain underrepresented in all those countries where data are collected. For migrants, ethnic minority groups, and refugees, the GRALE report provided a similar analysis of low participation rates (UIL, 2009, p. 67).

Not everything has been bleak, however. First, in civil society the International Council for Adult Education has enjoyed a resurgence of energy and effectiveness. Its international advocacy workshops for emerging leaders in adult education have supported a new generation of effective advocates for a rights-based adult learning agenda. Its women's network has been particularly effective. Its regional associations, like the Asia Pacific Bureau for Adult Education (ASPBAE), combine research and policy advice that have significant impacts on regional policies. It has also built alliances with civil society agencies more generally through the World Social Forum and the Global Campaign for Education. Through the first decade of the 21st century, it benefited from the experience and leadership of its president, Paul Bélanger, who was the chief architect of CONFINTEA V during his years at UNESCO.

Second, the period of uncertainty at the Hamburg Institute ended with the consolidation of the renamed UNESCO Institute for Lifelong Learning (UIL) as a full-fledged UNESCO Institute, which led to significant initiatives during the decade after the Hamburg conference. UIL played a central role in developments to strengthen the role of adult literacy and wider lifelong learning in Africa. It acted as the focal point for UNESCO in supporting literacy developments for young people and adults—but especially for girls and women more widely. UIL supported a dialogue between practitioners working with adult learners in prisons, culminating in the creation of a UNESCO chair for adult learning in prisons in Quebec. One successful development arising directly from CONFINTEA V was UIL's role in coordinating the spread of

New Directions for Adult and Continuing Education • DOI: 10.1002/ace

Adult Learners' Weeks and learning festivals as tools for motivation and engagement of underrepresented learners, and as vehicles for policy discussion in more than 50 countries. Its function as the continuing focal point for international dialogue is essential for the state and civil society cooperation needed to further the interests of adult learners.

Third, a number of transnational networks have emerged around common themes. Some, like PASCAL, the learning cities network, have shared experiences globally about effective ways of securing alliances across the social policy silos to create lifelong learning strategies for major urban conurbations. Other less formal networks, like the one for people with Parkinson's disease, have used the potential of the Internet to create communities of expert patients. More formal developments in open and distance learning, like Open Educational Resources and iTunes U, have made academic resources freely available for people with access to the technology and the language to make use of it (see www.oercommons.org, www.open.edu/itunes, www.projects .kmi.open.ac, www.itunes.ox.ac.uk, www.itunes.stanford.edu). Of course, the strides in new technology that empower many learners also reinforce the marginalization of the poorest and those who lack access to the technologies.

Overall, the reduction in commitment to adult learning has been uneven. The ebb and flow of commitment can be seen in regional developments. Within Europe the adoption of the 2000 Lisbon Agenda led, through the Grundtvig program for adult liberal education, to a major growth in transnational cooperation and exchange through projects involving partners in different countries (DVV, n.d.). Many initiatives have been designed to strengthen education for democratic citizenship, fuelled by the energy and enthusiasm of the relatively new democracies of central and southeastern Europe. Projects on outreach strategies, educational guidance for adults; good second language teaching; on the accreditation of prior learning and achievement; and on effective strategies to facilitate the settlement of migrants each led to effective if loosely organized networks of practitioners and policy makers.

In the university sector, research networks like the European Society for Research in the Education of Adults have strengthened comparative studies, and two European Masters programs in the Education of Adults have been established, each engaging multiple partners in different European countries. In the UK, the Wider Benefits of Learning Research Centre was complemented by a center researching the economic benefits of learning to strengthen the evidence base for the role of adult learning in wider social policy. Paid educational leave, trade union learning programs, and imaginative initiatives like Denmark's Job Rotation scheme abounded. Yet despite the evident strengthening of adult educators in the European community, the EU participation target for adult learning was not achieved. By the time of the strategy paper *EU 2020*, European policy makers, driven by concerns about global competitiveness and the consequences of banking and financial crises, had moved away from the *Hamburg Declaration*'s vision of a holistic approach towards a narrower and more instrumental focus on learning for economic growth (EU, 2000, 2010).

Impressive cooperation also exists between Asia and Europe through the intergovernmental Asia–Europe Meeting's (ASEM) Education and Research Hub for Lifelong Learning. This brings together universities, governments, and other civil society partners in interregional research and development initiatives, among them a concern with national strategies for lifelong learning to address barriers to participation and how these might best be overcome. Discussions have contributed to the adoption of legislation on lifelong learning in, for example, South Korea and Vietnam. Major advances in eradicating illiteracy have been accompanied by rapid expansion in lifelong learning in China. India, too, has developed enlightened legislation and an ambitious strategy for tackling the gender gap in literacy. Of course, good legislation and policies in themselves are not enough, as the example of Utter Pradesh highlights. There sustained and imaginative work by Nirantar, a women's voluntary organization, has ensured that rights of access to education secured in law can be exercised in practice by Dalit women in Lalitpur (see www.nirantar.net).

The increasing economic and political influence of Brazil, whose government has a dynamic and intimate dialogue with civil society organizations, helped to reenergize the state-civil society dialogue at the end of the first decade of the 21st century. Similar dialogues have developed in a number of Latin American countries, where popular education has, characteristically, developed without significant state financing. There has, too, been some loss of confidence in simply focusing development policies on growth. The emerging focus on well-being as a necessary focus for policy, the work of the Sarkozy Commission, and the study findings of *The Spirit Level* (Wilkinson & Pickett, 2009) all point to a need to find different measures of human development. Bhutan's insistence on measuring all new policies for their impact on happiness, Ecuador's adoption of the rights of mother Earth in its constitution, and widespread concern to rebalance ecological and economic policies all suggest that the space for creative spaces for adult learning are needed more than ever (Stiglitz, Sen, & Fitoussi, 2009).

Nevertheless, despite these positive indications, there can be no doubt that developments in adult learning since CONFINTEA V have been more heavily influenced by the OECD and World Bank agenda than by that elaborated in the *Hamburg Declaration* or *Learning: The Treasure Within*. Policies focused on learning for the labor market tend to concentrate on higher-paid and better-educated staff. They leave too many groups outside of the scope of publicly and privately supported programs. As the *Hamburg Declaration* recognized, inclusion relies not only on making access formally available but also on targeting additional resources to secure the participation of underrepresented groups. This analysis was endorsed immediately before CONFINTEA VI, when Brazil hosted the International Civil Society Forum (FISC). Organized by ICAE and a host of partner bodies, the proceedings highlighted the extent of the failure to achieve the CONFINTEA V aspirations, particularly for marginalized groups, and renewed the call for a rights-based approach to lifelong learning.

As we approach 2015, the 2011 EFA Global Monitoring Report provides graphic illustration of the consequences of this:

> The world is not on track to achieve the Education for All targets set for 2015. Although there has been progress in many areas, the overarching message to emerge from the 2011 EFA Global Monitoring Report is that most of the goals will be missed by a wide margin. Countries affected by armed conflict face particularly daunting challenges. Governments will have to demonstrate a far greater sense of urgency, resolve and common purpose to bring the targets within reach. (UNESCO, 2011, p.15)

Little at CONFINTEA VI in 2009 or at Rio+20 in 2012 gave confidence that governments share such urgency. Not enough of them recognize the key role adult learning can play in achieving a world in which everyone can live with dignity. As the United Nations embarks on decisions about what is to follow the Millenium Development Goals in 2015, advocates for adult learning and for the rights of all to education have a larger than ever task ahead of them in making their case for the value of learning as a good in itself and as a tool for the achievement of other policy goals.

References

Commission of the European Communities. (1993). *Growth, competitiveness, employment: The challenges and ways forward into the 21st century*. Brussels, Belgium: Author.

Daniel, J. (2003). *Advocating adult education—and then what?* Retrieved from http://portal .unesco.org/education/en/ev.php-URL_ID=22535&URL_DO=DO_TOPIC&URL_SEC TION=201.htm

Delors, J. (Ed.). (1996). *Learning: The treasure within*. Paris, France: UNESCO.

DVV. (n.d.). *International partnerships and solidarity in action*. Retrieved from http://www .iiz-dvv.de/index.php?article id=496&clang=1

European Union. (2000). *The Lisbon Special European Council (March 2000): Towards a Europe of innovation and knowledge*. Brussels, Belgium: Author.

European Union. (2010). *Europe 2020*. Brussels, Belgium: Author.

International Council for Adult Education (ICAE). (2003). *Agenda for the future—six years later*. Montevideo, Uruguay: Author.

International Council for Adult Education (ICAE). (2004). World Social Forum special double issue. *Convergence, XXXVI*(3/4).

Organization for Economic Cooperation and Development. (2007). *Understanding the social outcomes of learning*. Paris, France: Author.

Preston, J., & Green, A. (2003). *The macro-social benefits of education, training and skills in comparative perspective*. Research Report No. 9. London, England: Institute of Education, Centre for the Wider Benefits of Learning.

Schuller, T., Preston, J., Hammond, C., Brassett-Grundy, A., & Bynner, J. (2004). *The benefits of learning: The impact of education on health, family life and social capital*. London, England: Routledge.

Stiglitz, J., Sen, A., & Fitoussi, J.-P. (2009). *Report of the Commission on the Measurement of Economic Performance and Social Progress*. (The Sarkozy Commission). Retrieved from http://www.stiglitz-sen-fitoussi.fr/documents/rapport_anglais.pdf

UNESCO. (1997). *Hamburg Declaration on adult learning and agenda for the future*. Paris, France: Author.

UNESCO. (2000). *Education for all goals*. Retrieved from http://portal.unesco.org/education/en/ev.php-URL_ID=42579&URL_DO=DO_TOPIC&URL_SECTION=201.html

UNESCO. (2011). *The hidden crisis: Armed conflict and education*. EFA Global Monitoring Report. Retrieved from http://unesdoc.unesco.org/images/0019/001907/190743e.pdf

UNESCO Institute for Lifelong Learning (UIL). (2009). *Global report on adult learning and education*. Hamburg, Germany: Author.

United Nations. (2000a). *The millennium development goals*. Retrieved from http://www.undp.org/content/undp/en/home/mdgoverview.html

United Nations. (2000b). *The UN millennium declaration*. Retrieved from http://www.un.org/millennium/declaration/ares552e.pdf

United Nations. (2011). *The millennium development goals report 2011*. Retrieved from http://www.un.org/millenniumgoals/11_MDG%20Report_EN.pdf

Wilkinson, R., & Pickett, K. (2009). *The spirit level: Why equality is better for everyone*. London, England: Penguin.

ALAN TUCKETT *was elected president of the International Council for Adult Education in 2011. From 1988–2011 he was chief executive of the National Institute of Adult Continuing Education in England and Wales, where he launched Adult Learners' Week, now emulated in more than 50 countries.*

New Directions for Adult and Continuing Education • DOI: 10.1002/ace

8

This chapter considers Theme 9 of the Hamburg Declaration:
The economics of adult learning.

The Economics of Adult Education

Richard Desjardins

As the *Hamburg Declaration* makes clear, adult education (AE) is a key component of development strategies that seek to ensure the long-term well-being of
nations. Yet, with few exceptions most countries systematically underinvest in
AE. Of course, it is no easy task to achieve adequate investment levels that
reflect an appropriate balance between costs and benefits, account for market
failures, and distribute funds in ways consistent with human welfare. Apart from
political will, other major obstacles involve the lack of comparable data and the
difficulty in measuring the benefits of AE (OECD, 2007). In this chapter, I
assess the state of investment in AE by summarizing worldwide approaches to
financing AE, reviewing developments in the period between the 1997 and
2009 CONFINTEA conferences. I outline some key problems and constraints
and then suggest some ways we might improve matters.

Investment in AE

Financial support for AE varies greatly among countries. A variety of different
arrangements exist: some implicit, others more explicit, concerning who pays
for what and under which conditions. Thus, consistent, comparable, and reliable data on investment in AE is rarely available. In this section, I describe the
main approaches to funding and attempt to assess variations between countries and progress over time since the 1997 *Hamburg Declaration* (UNESCO,
1997).

Total investment in AE varies substantially between countries and
regions. One major source of difference is the higher level of investment by
nongovernment sources in high-income countries. Using Germany as an
example, Table 8.1 helps to put this into perspective.

NEW DIRECTIONS FOR ADULT AND CONTINUING EDUCATION, no. 138, Summer 2013 © 2013 Wiley Periodicals, Inc.
Published online in Wiley Online Library (wileyonlinelibrary.com) • DOI: 10.1002/ace.20056

Table 8.1. Total and public expenditures on AE, and public expenditures on education, Germany.

	GDP	Public expenditures on education		Total stakeholder expenditures for AE		Public expenditure on AE		
	Euros (000s)	Euros (000s)	% of GDP	Euros (000s)	% of GDP	Euros (000s)	% of GDP	% of public expenditures on education
2006	2,307,200,000	108,438,400	4.70%	24,100,000	1.04%	1,400,000	0.06%	1.29%
1996	1,876,180,000	86,304,280	4.60%	27,800,000	1.48%	1,500,000	0.08%	1.74%

Note: Figures for GDP and total expenditures on AE are from 1996 and 2006, but figures for public expenditures on education are from 1998 and 2003.

Sources: Total and public expenditures on AE (UNESCO, 2008f); public expenditures on education (World Bank, 2007).

Similar data from Denmark and Sweden show that their total spending on AE was about 1% and 4.9% of GDP in 1998, respectively, while in Spain it was about 0.4% in 2001 (OECD, 2003). These figures include public and private spending but are not comparable, because each country has a different concept of what to include. For example, the Swedish figures include in-service training, which partly explains why it dwarfs the others. Other estimates can include indirect spending, including foregone taxes, wage costs during training periods, and individual opportunity costs, which can be substantial. For example, Austria estimated its indirect spending on AE at about 1.2% of GDP in 2004 (UNESCO, 2008f).

Estimates over time suggest a lessening investment in AE in several high-income countries since 1997. As Table 8.1 shows, expenditure on AE is estimated to have fallen in Germany from about 1.5% of GDP in 1996 to about 1% in 2006. However, this trend should be interpreted with caution, because systematic accounting of AE expenditures does not exist and there are no standards or common definitions for establishing comparability. To put the scale of investment in AE into perspective, it is useful to contrast it with public expenditures on education overall. Average national expenditures on education were about 4% of GDP in 1998, increasing to about 5% in 2005 (World Bank, 2007). I now turn to examining various different funding sources.

Governments. National governments tend to invest about 1% of their public education budgets on AE, but wide variations exist and often the fraction is much smaller (Archer, 2007). Despite being too low, there are also signs of decrease. Table 8.1 shows that public expenditure in Germany fell from about 1.7% in 1996 to about 1.3% in 2006. Other countries are not so generous: the European Commission has expressed concern about the sharp decline of public expenditures on AE among countries recently admitted to membership (UNESCO, 2008f). In Nordic countries, government spending on AE is higher, in line with their higher participation rates, especially among disadvantaged groups. For example, Finland's government spent close to 0.6% of GDP on AE in 2001, which was about 9.5% of its public expenditures on education (OECD, 2003). Countries featuring high public spending on AE explicitly recognize the public good aspects of AE as well as the need for public intervention to maintain a high standard of equity.

However, despite evidence for the public benefits of AE (Feinstein & Hammond, 2004; McMahon, 1999; Schuller, Preston, Hammond, Brassett-Grundy, & Bynner, 2004), skepticism remains high, particularly among countries with governments that do not view adult education as a matter for public policy. Countries like the Czech Republic, Kyrgyzstan, and Poland tend not to regard AE as a public good and ignore the critical role it can play in building consensus, maintaining democratic institutions, and fostering social cohesion. In low and lower middle income countries, the expansion of primary education and the growing demand for secondary education also place enormous pressures on public investment in AE (UNESCO, 2008a). For example, India estimates that it spends a miniscule 0.02% of its education budget on AE, even as it attempts to run the largest literacy campaign in the world (UNESCO, 2008c). Many other developing countries in Asia and the Pacific spend closer to 1% (Soliven & Reyes, 2008). In Africa, Gambia spent about 0.3% of its education budget on AE, Kenya 0.3–0.4%, Malawi 0.5%, Senegal 1%, South Africa 1%, and Zambia 0.2% (UNESCO, 2008g). Overall, levels of investment in AE are inadequate for meeting the challenges that low-income countries are facing. Estimates indicate that in order to eradicate illiteracy in a sustainable way, at least 3% of education budgets should be committed to literacy programs plus a further 3% for other AE programs (Global Campaign for Education, 2005). For example, Cape Verde is the only African country spending anywhere near the recommended amount, with estimates of their public spending reaching 8.7% (UNESCO, 2008g).

Civil Society. Very little systematic information is available regarding investment by nongovernment organizations (NGOs) even though they play an important role in the provision of AE. Civil society contributions are particularly widespread in low- and middle-income countries, but are also present in high-income countries. For example, Australia reports it has over 1,200 nonprofit community-based providers (UNESCO, 2008e). NGOs can also be major funders and providers: in Cameroon, NGOs fund 95% of that country's AE; in Senegal, 45% (UNESCO, 2008g). Contributions can include offering space, volunteers, materials, and other in-kind contributions including offering courses. Indeed, many government-funded programs rely on charity from civil society, particularly in the form of volunteers who act as facilitators and instructors. The impressive success of India's literacy campaign can be attributed to a mobilization of large numbers of volunteers. Similarly, in Bangladesh, Brazil, and other countries, instructors in AE are paid either very low salaries or none at all. This reflects the temporary nature of AE programs in many countries and the lack of appropriate governance and provision structures. However, while important, an exclusive reliance on volunteers is unsustainable, especially in regard to program quality. Paying low salaries, if any, to practitioners keeps AE costs artificially low. So does the use of public facilities. However, the latter is an example of good practice in sharing, coordinating, and using available resources, because it does not have serious adverse consequences on quality and sustainability.

Employers. Employer involvement in providing AE and as a source of demand is growing, especially among high-income countries. Investments are made to upgrade and re-skill workers so as to remain competitive in globalized product and service markets. The highest training activity seems to be concentrated in firms that are large, competing in global markets and undergoing significant technological and organizational change (OECD, 2003). Increases in job-related AE explain much of the rise in AE in high-income countries since the early 1980s. Available comparative data (mostly from OECD countries) shows that about two out of every three persons who undertake AE do so with some employer support, implying that employers are the most common source of support for AE (Desjardins, Rubenson, & Milana,

good data on AE. Although employers have an incentive to invest in AE, they are also under pressure to control costs, especially in competitive environments. In the absence of appropriate incentives, some firms choose low skills strategies to compete in product and service markets (Brown, Green, & Lauder, 2001). Individuals, especially the most vulnerable, are also constrained, principally by limited earnings but also by the risk of losing their jobs. Investment is thus highly dependent on the perception of what benefits will be gained and by whom. Combined with poor information, these conditions often mean that priority is given to other activities. Indeed, AE remains marginal and underfunded, especially in low- and middle-income countries.

Third, there is a universal low commitment to and low priority for AE. Countries around the globe differ markedly in whether they have a strategy to ensure adequate resources for AE. They also differ in their priorities, pace of progress, and the availability of information for assessing progress. Many mandates to improve AE structures remain unfunded and neglected, and they often receive low priority in public budgets. Budgeted funds are sometimes not released because they are kept as an option and are released only if other priorities are met. In developing countries, this means AE funds are often diverted to compensate for shortfalls in the primary or secondary education budget. This problem can be exacerbated when budgetary processes are decentralized, because some communities may be more susceptible to financial strain or their priorities may diverge from central government policies. Even in high-income countries, where there is universal primary education and high rates of upper secondary completion, levels of investment in AE are still too low (OECD, 2003).

Fourth, government support tends to go to those already better off. Many governments recognize a role for public investment in AE, either for correcting market failures or for redressing social disadvantages. But unless government support is carefully designed, it tends to go to adults who already participate in AE. When properly targeted, government support can reach those adults most in need, but only if funds are earmarked and complemented with outreach activities. Often this approach is more expensive, and support rarely reaches adults in need. This is especially the case when market or quasi-market mechanisms are used. Programs requiring individuals to apply with eligibility criteria to qualify are equally divisive. Enforcing accountability measures for use of public funds by NGOs can lead to barriers for disadvantaged groups, because it encourages them to recruit those most likely to succeed. Unless funds are earmarked for specific groups, even AE initiatives with pronounced ambitions to reach disadvantaged adults can provide a service that corresponds better to the demands of the advantaged.

Fifth, private sources show a lack of incentive to invest. For many countries, progress depends on their ability to mobilize private resources to supplement public funding in AE. But many employers and individuals lack the incentives to invest. In some cases, employers are reluctant if the skills to be gained are general, because their employees may then become more employable at competing firms, and the sponsoring firm may lose its investment. In practice, many firms choose to invest in general skills anyway because it is difficult to distinguish general from specific skills. Several other labor-market imperfections exist, but incentives remain poorly aligned. Incentive problems are being handled in diverse ways. Favorable tax treatments are commonly used through outlays such as levy systems that promote AE. Nevertheless, policies that comprehensively address incentive problems and other market failures are often lacking and in many cases remain entirely absent.

Sixth, incentive strategies exacerbate inequalities. Where incentive strategies do exist, they tend to rely on quasi-market-based approaches that exacerbate inequalities. When incentives are directed at employers and individuals without targeted strategies, they can serve to exacerbate inequalities. Unfortunately, there appears to be a lack of willingness in policy circles to address directly the implications of the increasing impact of employer funding on the distribution of AE. It is often politically infeasible to expect public sources to cover new demands, and the private sector is encouraged to contribute toward AE. But evidence suggests that there is a strong role for the public sector, particularly if issues of equity are involved.

In sum, the best approach to correct for market failures and inequities is structural reform; for example, through redefining public-private sector boundaries in the AE sector and aligning the incentives to invest. However, for many reasons this proves difficult. First, many of the failures are due to natural imperfections that are difficult to overcome, and no viable strategies to address them have yet been devised. Rarely do the funding mechanisms devised to implement government strategies genuinely address the nature of the problem (as, for example, inequality) or the forces that drive it. Doing this requires in-depth and ongoing public policy analysis, which requires technical capacity as well as well-established and responsive governances and provision structures in AE. Second, some imperfections of reform do not relate solely to AE, so reforms should not be undertaken without consideration of relevant trade-offs with other sectors. For example, imperfections may be linked to initial education structures that promote narrow vocational pathways or to occupational and industrial structures that may encourage a low skills equilibrium in the economy (Brown et al., 2001). Accordingly, it is necessary to coordinate approaches across policy sectors, both private and public.

Ways Forward

Although the situation seems dire, there are still several options for moving forward. Resources can be better mobilized. Demand and incentives to invest among stakeholders can be better fostered. These could include tax and institutional arrangements that favor cost sharing and promote cofinancing schemes that channel resources from at least two parties. Also, a stronger role for public funding could be asserted. Although nongovernmental resources need to be mobilized, public authorities also need to renew commitments to increase targeted funding for disadvantaged groups. Governments need to assert a stronger role in devising policies that comprehensively address market failures. Market-based principles cannot solve everything. Focusing only on regulatory and institutional arrangements that are conducive to enhancing investments by firms and individuals, as is the trend in many high-income countries, is not enough, especially if growing inequalities and under-investment are to be avoided.

Government support for disadvantaged groups could be complemented with targeting strategies. These include special outreach, guidance activities, and the earmarking of funds for certain groups. Such measures are based on the assumption that certain groups must use a certain proportion of the funds made available. The most significant challenge is to stimulate the demands among those groups for which the measures are taken. Adult education should be integrated into a broader development and poverty reduction strategy. Publicly funded AE has a strong role to play in preventing and alleviating adverse conditions, such as unemployment and large-scale displacements associated with modernization and other structural changes. This is equally applicable to community development in low- and middle-income countries. Rather than passive transfers of aid to individuals, communities, or nations, a renewed commitment to AE as a mechanism for activating development is needed. AE should be a central element of any development strategy and feature more prominently in poverty reduction strategy papers (PRSP).

NGOs are important for providing AE but lack recognition. They require adequate public funding and government support. This sector is more flexible and thus adapts to new demands faster than the formal system does. Also, it seems to reach adults who would otherwise not enroll in AE. The integration of the voluntary sector into a comprehensive AE policy can be successful only if direct state intervention is avoided but public funds are provided. Bureaucratic barriers that prevent operation or access to funds need to be removed. As long as it fulfills the goals for which state funding is received, the sector must be left to develop its own strategies. At the same time, a mechanism for coordination and information sharing is essential. Rarely is there effective coordination among the many NGOs that are operating in a given area. A lack of coordination leads to inefficiencies, such as parallel structures of provision, even though there are clear advantages to sharing facilities and staff. Collaboration between providers can cut program development costs and may allow for a more efficient use of accommodations and equipment.

Finally, it is necessary to adopt a sustainable strategy to develop AE, in which public investment is adequate, consistent, and proportionate to GDP over the long run. This includes the need for continuous policy and institutional development. Developing a diversified, integrated, and holistic AE sector requires sustained investment. This can only happen with concrete political commitments at all levels. External aid should be seen only as a way to achieve accelerated progress in this respect.

References

Archer, D. (2007). Financing of adult education. *Convergence, XL*(3–4), 253–256.

Brown, P., Green, A., & Lauder, H. (2001). *High skills: Globalization, competitiveness, and skill formation.* Oxford, England: Oxford University Press.

Desjardins, R., Rubenson, K., & Milana, M. (2006). *Unequal chances to participate in adult learning: International perspectives.* Paris, France: UNESCO International Institute of Educational Planning.

Feinstein, L., & Hammond, C. (2004). The contribution of adult learning to health and social capital. *Oxford Review of Education, 30*(2), 199–221.

Global Campaign for Education. (2005). *Writing the wrongs: International benchmarks on adult literacy.* London, England: ActionAid International.

McMahon, W. (1999). *Education and development: Measuring the social benefits.* Oxford, England: Oxford University Press.

OECD. (2003). *Beyond rhetoric: Adult learning policies and practices.* Paris, France: Author.

OECD. (2007). *Understanding the social outcomes of learning.* Paris, France: CERI.

Rubenson, K. (1999). Supply of lifelong learning opportunities. In A. Tuijnman & T. Schuller (Eds.), *Lifelong learning policy and research: Proceedings of an international symposium* (pp. 109–120). London, England: Portland Press.

Schuller, T., Preston, J., Hammond, C., Brassett-Grundy, A., & Bynner, J. (2004). *The benefits of learning: The impact of education on health, family life and social capital.* London, England: Routledge Falmer.

Soliven, P. S., & Reyes, M. A. N. (2008). *The development and state of the art of adult learning and education: National report of the Republic of Phillipines.* Retrieved from http://www.unesco.org/uil/en/nesico/confintea/confinteanatrep.html

UNESCO. (1997). *The Hamburg Declaration on adult learning and agenda for the future.* Paris, France: Author.

UNESCO. (2008a). *Education for all by 2015, will we make it?* EFA Global Monitoring Report. Paris, France: Author.

UNESCO. (2008b). *Georgia national report.* Hamburg, Germany: Author.

UNESCO. (2008c). *India national report.* Hamburg, Germany: Author.

UNESCO. (2008d). *Senegal national report.* Hamburg, Germany: Author.

UNESCO. (2008e). *Synthesis report for Asia Pacific region.* Hamburg, Germany: Author.

UNESCO. (2008f). *Synthesis report for Europe and North America region.* Hamburg, Germany: Author.

UNESCO. (2008g). *Synthesis report for Sub-Saharan Africa region.* Hamburg, Germany: Author.

UNESCO. (2008h). *Tanzania national report.* Hamburg, Germany: Author.

UNESCO. (2009). *Overcoming equality: Why governance matters.* EFA Global Monitoring Report. Paris, France: Author.

World Bank. (2007). *World Development Indicators Online.* Retrieved from http://go.world bank.org/3JU2HA60D0

RICHARD DESJARDINS is an associate professor in the department of education at Aahus University in Denmark.

New Directions for Adult and Continuing Education • DOI: 10.1002/ace

9

This chapter reaffirms the necessity of rekindling the hope and promise of the Hamburg Declaration.

Whither Utopia?

Tom Nesbit

The *Hamburg Declaration on Adult Learning and Agenda for the Future* (UNESCO, 1997) is perhaps the most utopian statement about adult learning and education (ALE) in recent times. Grounded in the ideas of radical educators Paulo Freire and Ivan Illich, it built upon two earlier influential and inspiring reports (Delors, 1996; Faure, 1972) that promoted general adherence to the values of helping to build a sustainable world, promote peace, celebrate diversity, and defend human rights. Deliberately adopting an extensive definition of adult education, the statement portrayed its complex spectrum under 10 themes. Each theme has been fully explored in the previous chapters as well as in the *Global Report on Adult Learning and Education* (GRALE; UNESCO Institute for Lifelong Learning, 2009a), discussed throughout the CONFINTEA VI conference in Belém and at the International Civil Society Forum (FISC) held immediately before it and updated in the *Belém Framework for Action* (UNESCO Institute for Lifelong Learning, 2009b). Descriptive and thoughtful reflections on these discussions can be found in special editions of three journals: *Adult Learning* (Alfred, 2011), *Adult Education and Development* (Hinzen, 2010), and the *International Review of Education* (Medel-Añonuevo, Torres, & Desjardins, 2011b).

However, the scope and power of the *Hamburg Declaration* also require a more deliberate analysis than can be achieved in country reports or international conference discussions, which necessitate a degree of consensus and agreement among participants and so tend to generate conservative proposals and statements. Analysis of the previous chapters demonstrates that the utopian ideals and goals of the *Hamburg Declaration* are still far from being achieved. The world is certainly no more peaceful or safer than it was in 1997. Inequalities continue to grow. Economic crises have both proliferated and deepened, threatening democratic and financial systems the world over. Although

NEW DIRECTIONS FOR ADULT AND CONTINUING EDUCATION, no. 138, Summer 2013 © 2013 Wiley Periodicals, Inc.
Published online in Wiley Online Library (wileyonlinelibrary.com) • DOI: 10.1002/ace.20057

some of the most egregious cases of human rights abuse are now better known and finally being challenged, there is still much that remains. Diversity is now more widely acknowledged and respected in principle, although it remains elusive in practice and nationalisms are again resurging. Environmental sustainability, now more commonly understood, is still poorly and erratically implemented. Work and workplaces have been so affected by technological innovations and economic uncertainty that jobs are increasingly shifted from developed to less-developed (that is, cheaper) countries while workers' rights and benefits and their organizations remain under constant siege.

In addition, adult education has faced its own challenges. Misunderstood (too frequently confused with literacy, basic education, or lifelong learning) and often marginalized in educational and political circles, the field has made questionable advances since 1997. As Agostino (2010) acutely observes, adult education "is one of those fields where everybody seems to agree that it is important but not many people are actually interested in providing the support it requires in order for it to be implemented as a human right" (p. 460). This is clearly evident in the policy and research arenas, where adult education is "traditionally and chronically neglected and under-prioritized" (Medel-Añonuevo, Torres, & Desjardins, 2011a, p. 6).

Of course, adult education is regarded and constrained differently in different countries. Although virtually all nations emphasize the education of young people as a central institution of their societies, they regard the education of adults far less favorably. In Chapter 8 of this volume, Desjardins notes that countries rarely agree upon one definition of adult education, often underestimate its benefits, and systematically underfund it. Further, "state institutions are not homogeneous, and adult education programmes take place across several units, departments, secretaries, or even ministries, very often competing for resources and recognition and making institutional collaboration difficult if not impossible" (Torres, 2011, p. 48). Thus, the marginality, convoluted organization, and inadequate financing of adult education render it vulnerable to shifts in political influence, so it cannot be (or seem to be) overly critical of those who support it fiscally or politically.

And yet, as the *Hamburg Declaration* makes clear, adult education can continue to play a critical role in the development of societies. Adult education is often the first place that people systematically encounter others' ideas or those that challenge mainstream notions. It can also facilitate the development of a critical consciousness that fosters people's understandings of their past, present, and future, and it can encourage them to appreciate and act to redress inequalities. This remains as true in 2013 as in 1997. Of course countries have distinctive approaches to adult education and different capacities to act. As they change their perspectives over time, we must be careful not to apply the same standards universally. However, the *Hamburg Declaration* clearly puts forward a set of collective ideals that all can strive toward, regardless of circumstance.

The earlier chapters suggest several common issues that I want to address further. The first concerns the political dimensions of adult education—an aspect that lies at the heart of the *Hamburg Declaration* and fundamentally shapes the contexts in which adult education takes place. The roles of institutional actors are key, and I next explore the contributions of various types of organizations in shaping ALE policies and discourse. From a review of the developments since CONFINTEA V, it is easy to conclude that there is little confidence that the goals of the *Hamburg Declaration* will be realized any time soon. Yet one task of progressive educators is to unveil opportunities for hope, no matter the obstacles (Freire, 2004). In that vein, I list some of the more positive changes that have taken place since 1997 and conclude with some suggestions about how to reaffirm and reenergize the hope and promise of the *Hamburg Declaration*.

Adult Education's Political Dimensions

Most authors in this volume identify a noticeable change between the rhetorics of CONFINTEA V and VI; to wit, "the political edge" (Stromquist, Chapter 3 of this volume, p. 33) has been taken off. As they note, the Hamburg conference happened during a period of rapid change, filled with anger at the world's injustices but infused with hope and enthusiasm for the possibilities of transforming civil society and adult education. Regrettably, this passion now seems to have waned; expectations have fragmented and weakened in a more precarious age of uncertainty and instability. Capitalism now seems part of the established order, and there is much greater accommodation of, and adherence to, the strictures of neoliberalism. Issues of peace, justice, and human rights have become subjugated to economic viability. Adult education itself now seems to focus less on the aspirations of what it can be and more on documenting and monitoring the planning, implementation, or evaluation of what currently exists. Throughout the myriad descriptions of the "what" and the "how" of adult education, there is correspondingly too little attention on "why." Rarely is there much sense of the *Hamburg Declaration's* (or any other) overarching vision of adult education or concern for how broader issues or macropolitical and cultural realities might be addressed.

For example, most of the country reports collected in the GRALE do not refer to or reflect upon the national and international political issues that have marked the beginning of the 21st century. The rise of global terrorism; the rapid increase in and effects of economic globalization; the growing gap between rich and poor; rising unemployment (particularly among women, young people, and immigrants); the drift toward various fundamentalisms and ethnic bigotry; continuing hostilities in the Middle East; highly visible wars in Iraq and Afghanistan (and a few other conflicts not so conspicuous); the demise of the Soviet Union; genocide in Rwanda and "ethnic cleansing" in Sudan and the former Yugoslavia; continuing famines, pandemics, and disease; transnational migration; the rights of indigenous people and minorities;

New Directions for Adult and Continuing Education • DOI: 10.1002/ace

recent environmental disasters; and a selective concern for the democratic and human rights of others hardly merit a mention. Even though the country reports were designed to focus on national approaches to ALE, why did they not mention such issues, even tangentially? Are such concerns irrelevant to government approaches to ALE?

Further, among all the calls upon adult education to help strengthen civil society, address pressing social issues, or reengage with a social mission, there is often too little sense of how to achieve such goals or to analyze specific examples of existing achievement. Perhaps, as Tuckett explains in Chapter 7, it all boils down to the interplay of two distinct and competing visions of ALE: "one vision grounded in human rights and focused on inclusiveness [and] the expansion of equal access and achievement; the other vision focused on learning useful for the labor market as a key component in human capital, itself central to economic growth" (p. 71). These two visions and the differences between them can be seen most clearly in the *Hamburg Declaration* on the one hand and by the statements and policies on education produced by the Organisation for Economic and Community Development (OECD), the International Monetary Fund, and the World Bank on the other. As Torres (2011) claims, this latter approach is marked by a "strong drive towards privatisation, decentralisation, accountability, and testing, [and] presenting an instrumental and economic model of educational policy and planning" (p. 46).

Of course, while differing values and perspectives should be encouraged and debated, domination by a narrow instrumental focus on adult education for economic growth presents a clear threat to realizing the *Hamburg Declaration*. Indeed, there is some evidence that this is already happening. For example, both the U.S. and Canadian country reports prepared for CONFINTEA VI appear as standard bureaucratic products that provide detailed but bland descriptions of state and provincial government-sponsored adult education and the extent of federal initiatives (Charters, 2011; Hill et al., 2008; Rubenson & Nesbit, 2011). Their lack of information on or discussion about the adult education provided by NGOs and civil society groups, their disregard for learners' perspectives, and the absence of any meta-analysis is striking. No attempts are made to identify any particular strengths or weaknesses in the current systems, situate current approaches in any historical or socio-political context, or suggest where improvements might occur. This is entirely consistent with OECD's overall approach, which tends to encourage an emphasis on certain aspects of ALE (such as state functions and approaches) while downplaying others (such as critical reflexivity, social change, or learner participation).

Organizational Roles in Policy Formation

Although there are certainly competing visions of what adult education can and should be, ideas need people and organizations to implement them. Here, the separate and intersecting roles of UNESCO, national governments, and civil society groups come into play. Certainly UNESCO intended that the development of the country reports that formed the basis of GRALE would contribute to a revival of national debates on ALE. To foster greater participation of civil society groups, it encouraged its national commissions to consult widely and hold inclusive conferences on draft versions of the reports. These conferences would discuss (and hopefully confirm) the reports' findings and, in so doing, create national dialogues involving governmental, nongovernmental, public, and private actors, including trade unions, social partners, and bilateral and multilateral development agencies (UNESCO Institute for Lifelong Learning, 2007).

Governments, who had the key responsibility for drafting the country reports, naturally participated in this process, if not always enthusiastically. Their reluctance stems in part from the organizational complexity mentioned earlier by Torres (2011) and their unwillingness to grant too much scope to civil society organizations but also perhaps because they did not wish to see their relative inaction highlighted. As the GRALE report makes clear, "many national government education and social policies have not prioritised adult learning and education as had been expected and hoped for following the *Hamburg Declaration*" (UNESCO Institute for Lifelong Learning, 2009a, p. 24).

Other participants, such as NGOs and civil society groups, were more welcoming of an opportunity to join these policy discussions. Most countries have one or more NGOs devoted to the promotion and coordination of various aspects of ALE and several more with a vested interest in it. Of course, such groups differ in their perspectives. In some cases the group plays "an entirely apolitical part as deliverers of services that critics believe are the job of the State, thereby it appears colluding in rather than challenging undesirable practices," while in others it assumes "a critical and even oppositional role, challenging the State from a basis of value and principle in terms of equity and redistribution" (Duke & Hinzen, 2006, p. 145). Specifically, those who advocate for social and educational transformation have generally struggled to survive in increasingly harsh and uncertain climates. In addition, they are often fragmented, poorly funded, and extremely reliant upon client, volunteer, and learner support. Consequently, they are severely constrained in their ability to develop sustainable programming, conduct any research other than the most basic information-gathering, and influence policy-formation For these reasons, NGOs are often prevented from addressing more systemic issues, promoting their interests widely, or challenging the prevailing ideologies of individualism, managerialism, and neoliberalism. So, the efforts of UNESCO and other organizations (like the International Council for Adult Education) to unite them, link their efforts, and advocate for their concerns are crucial; their support can produce major benefits far exceeding what each group can do alone. That said, the national conference approach met with mixed success in addressing and reasserting the *Hamburg Declaration*'s democratic and humanistic vision of adult education. In some countries, civil society participation was embraced enthusiastically (and certainly enlivened the

FISC preconference), while in others it was far more muted (Haddad, 2011; Rubenson & Nesbit, 2011).

The CONFINTEA conferences themselves are designed to corral these varied organizations and opinions under one UNESCO umbrella to produce consensus-driven policy directives. In an exploration of the creation and diffusion of global policies on lifelong learning, Jakobi (2012) provides an interesting perspective on this process. She suggests that world politics is increasingly based on a shared global culture and that organizations like UNESCO provide an expedient structure for the dissemination of policy ideas between countries. Thus different countries increasingly come to rely on the same principles and values, and global forums like CONFINTEA encourage and support both these principles and the process of their dissemination. Countries are considered more acceptable if they portray similar characteristics and policies as others (particularly the more powerful). International organizations like UNESCO can thus be regarded as crucial instruments for transnational forces to promote a hegemonic and consensus-making order of policy development.

Both Jakobi's (2012) analysis and the GRALE report suggest that an international consensus on lifelong learning is growing and that an increasing number of countries are trying to reform their education systems in order to accommodate it. However, as indicators for lifelong learning reform are too broad and ill-defined, there is a clear separation between the discourses of lifelong learning and any corresponding activities, which can be influenced by other factors. For example, Jakobi notes that national wealth significantly increases a country's probability of adopting lifelong learning reforms; poorer countries are less likely to initiate reforms than richer ones. In addition, it appears that the influence of international communities and organizations has increased. Globalization has provided bodies like the OECD, the World Bank, and the European Union with increased power. This has had, to date, two effects: first, the national characteristics of adult education policies and lifelong learning have become less distinctive. Second, education policies appear to be increasingly subordinate to the requirements of economic competitiveness and to be steered by prevailing economic interests.

Overall, this does not bode well for the broad implementation of the *Hamburg Declaration*'s goals. Although international organizations like UNESCO can be successful in reasserting, disseminating, and gaining acceptance for the ideas of the *Hamburg Declaration,* establishing common goals is very different from realizing them. Poor and already marginalized people (and the organizations that represent or advocate for them) have little effect on national policies, and in any case existing policy-implementation mechanisms have remained largely unchanged. So, given the limited capacity of NGOs and other civil society groups to influence national approaches, their efforts may well continue to be most productive in prolonging their lobbying efforts until their international organization and links become stronger.

Positive Changes

And yet, some positive changes since 1997 continue to offer hope. The *Hamburg Declaration* is couched so distinctively because CONFINTEA V was the first UNESCO-sponsored adult education conference to welcome and include civil society groups. Since then, UNESCO has continued to promote the increased involvement of NGOs and other civil society groups concerned with adult education. This has led directly to some governments extending their adult education policies and legislation, a few even enshrining them in their constitutions, and a significant number endorsing the document prepared by FISC, the International Civil Society Forum.

As the earlier chapters identify, there have been further benefits. In Chapter 1, Welton suggests that a "new imaginary" (p. 17) has broken into the Middle East, potentially spreading to the rest of the world and enabling us to learn to coexist and establish bonds of solidarity. In Chapter 2, Wagner identifies new ideas about and enhanced appreciation of literacy issues and a concern for greater quality (an issue also endorsed by Stromquist in Chapter 3). Stromquist also mentions the particular advantages of women-led NGOs in challenging narrow classifications of learning outcomes and the continued transmission of traditional but disempowering values. She also notes approvingly that the circumstances of women throughout the world are now more closely embedded in the wider and general principle of human rights. In Chapter 4, Rose explores the development of learning regions, an approach that she describes as embodying the best ideals of the *Hamburg Declaration*. In discussing environmental and ecological awareness in Chapter 5, Clover and Hill observe heightened attention to issues of sustainable development and climate change, citing the rise of Green parties in several countries and the closer linking of environmental concerns with other issues of human rights. Dinevski and Radovan in Chapter 6 chart the dramatic increase in the use of information and communication technologies, especially in social and educational settings. As they claim, the growth of e-learning has created new concepts and widened access to educational resources and enhanced opportunities for everyone to access and create knowledge. In Chapter 7, Tuckett notes that major international organizations like the International Council for Adult Education (ICEA) have enjoyed a resurgence of energy and enthusiasm, and ICEA's regional associations have built alliances with similar groups to impact regional policies, especially in Southeast Asia. UNESCO, too, has strengthened the roles of adult literacy and lifelong learning in Africa, particularly among women and young people. It has promoted adult education for adults in prison and has created chairs in this area and in community-based research and social responsibility of higher education. International Adult Learners' Weeks and related learning festivals now take place in over 50 countries. Several transnational networks—such as PASCAL, concerned with developing learning regions and cities—have emerged, and within Europe the success of research programs like Grundtvig have led to increased international cooperation and the parallel development of a new adult education academic journal (see www.rela.ep.liu.se). All these examples provide opportunities to rekindle the hopes and promise of the *Hamburg Declaration*, thereby holding out the possibility of a future that we want, rather than one dictated to us.

What Next?

Currently educational reforms depend upon government policies and the will and capacity to implement them. The *Hamburg Declaration on Adult Learning and Agenda for the Future* is merely a statement that requires others to animate it. So, as others claim, what is needed most now is less planning and more action—an approach implicit in the adoption of "From Rhetoric to Action" as the motto of CONFINTEA VI. Of course, as Medel-Añonuevo and colleagues (2011a) caution, we cannot expect

> the whole world of policy to be transformed in the direction of critical thinking and critical theory. But at least we may hope that blind technocratic orientations or policies based on bureaucratic and authoritarian rationality in adult education might become the exception rather than the rule. (p. 3)

In a world marked by rapid change, fundamental issues like justice or equality can become obscured. Also, as the polarizations between rich and poor and between privilege and oppression grow ever wider, these problems can easily become regarded as someone else's responsibility. Yet we live in an interconnected world; we are all (well, the 99% of us) in it together. This simple fact animates the drives for greater democracy and accountability and the demonstrations against financial and political institutions described by Welton in Chapter 1.

There is a common view that people living under difficult situations come to accept their fate because they can imagine no reasonable alternative. Others argue that the state has the responsibility to ensure that its citizens are prepared and able to make well-informed choices. Although apparently contrasting, both views corroborate the enduring relevance of adult education and the continuing importance of statements like the *Hamburg Declaration*. Adult education is a fundamental human right—not only in itself but also because it is vital for realizing other human rights. It has long championed commitment to a broader sense of social purpose rather than individualism, material acquisition, competition, or self-interest. It has also, throughout its history, demonstrated that no matter how bad things might get, people can always intervene, usually collectively, to improve them. What is possible is shaped, in part, by our visions. The greatest threats to realizing utopia come not just from government inaction but also from cynicism and passivity among us all. So we must strive to rekindle the "optimism of the will" that Gramsci (1971, p. 175) claimed as essential to creating a new kind of global order and genuine social and economic change.

Current economic, environmental, and political crises clearly require us to reconstruct societies along more democratic, egalitarian, and rational lines. Better than any other recent calls to arms, the *Hamburg Declaration* still offers that utopian ideal; the rest, however, is up to us. My friend and fellow Canadian adult educator, Budd Hall, who did as much as anyone else to craft the *Hamburg Declaration*, quotes from the *Faber Book of Utopias*: "Anyone who is capable of love must at some time have wanted the world to be a better place, for we all want our loved ones to live free of suffering, injustice and heartbreak" (Carey, 1999, p. 1). As Hall (2009) puts it, "We have the right to a new utopian vision, a vision that responds to the collective needs of the majority of persons in the world, not simply the few." However, he adds, we also "need to grasp the power of the utopic vision for ourselves" (p. 197). To use an old popular education expression: "We dig where we stand."

References

Agostino, A. (2010). CONFINTEA VI: Lifelong learning for sustainability. *Development, 53*(4), 460–464.

Alfred, M. (Ed.). (2011). *Adult Learning, 22*(4).

Carey, J. (Ed.). (1999). *The Faber book of utopias*. London, England: Faber.

Charters, A. N. (2011). Reflections on involvement with six UNESCO international conferences on adult education and suggestions for the future. *Adult Learning, 22*(4)–23(1), 14–17.

Delors, J. (1996). *Learning: The treasure within. Report to UNESCO of the International Commission on Education for the Twenty-First Century*. Paris, France: UNESCO.

Duke, C., & Hinzen, H. (2006). Basic and continuing adult education policies. *Adult Education and Development, 66*, 131–167.

Faure, E. (1972). *Learning to be: The world of education today and tomorrow*. Paris, France: UNESCO.

Freire, P. (2004). *Pedagogy of hope: Reliving pedagogy of the oppressed*. New York, NY: Continuum International Publishing Group.

Gramsci, A. (1971). *Selections from the prison notebooks* (G. M. Smith, Trans.). New York, NY: International Publishers.

Haddad, S. (2011). Civil society participation at CONFINTEA VI. *Adult Learning, 22*(4), 34–39.

Hall, B. L. (2009). The right to a new Utopia: Adult learning and the changing world of work in an era of global capitalism. In R. Maclean & D. Wilson (Eds.), *International handbook of education for the changing world of work* (pp. 97–110). Dordrecht, Netherlands: Springer.

Hill, R. J., Daigle, E. A., Graybeal, L., Walker, W., Avalon, C., Fowler, N., & Massey, M. W. (2008). *A review and critique of the 2008 United States National Report on the Development and State of the Art of Adult Learning and Education (ALE)*. ERIC Document Reproduction Service No. ED537666.

Hinzen, H. (Ed.). (2010). *Adult Education & Development, 75*.

Jakobi, A. P. (2012). International organisations and policy diffusion: The global norm of lifelong learning. *Journal of International Relations and Development, 15*(1), 31–64.

Medel-Añonuevo, C., Torres, C. A., & Desjardins, R. (2011a). CONFINTEA VI follow-up: The challenges of moving from rhetoric to action. *International Review of Education, 57*(1–2), 1–8.

Medel-Añonuevo, C., Torres, C. A., & Desjardins, R. (Eds.). (2011b). *International Review of Education, 57*(1–2).

Rubenson, K., & Nesbit, T. (2011). CONFINTEA VI from a Canadian perspective. *International Review of Education, 57*(1–2), 127–143.

Torres, C. A. (2011). Dancing on the deck of the Titanic? Adult education, the nation-state, and new social movements. *International Review of Education, 57*(1–2), 39–55.

UNESCO. (1997). *The Hamburg Declaration on adult learning and agenda for the future.* Paris, France: Author.

UNESCO Institute for Lifelong Learning. (2007). *Guidelines for the preparation of national reports on the situation of adult learning and education.* Hamburg, Germany: Author.

UNESCO Institute for Lifelong Learning. (2009a). *Global report on adult learning and education.* Hamburg, Germany: Author.

UNESCO Institute for Lifelong Learning. (2009b). *Harnessing the power and potential of adult learning and education for a viable future: Belém framework for action.* Hamburg, Germany: Author.

TOM NESBIT *has recently retired from Simon Fraser University in Vancouver, BC, where he was associate dean of lifelong learning. He is a member of the educational sectoral council of the Canadian Commission for UNESCO.*

INDEX